WATER DAMAGE

P9-DNZ-244

8W

Dear Reader:

The book you are about to read is the latest bestseller from the St. Martin's True Crime Library, the imprint *The New York Times* calls "the leader in true crime!" The True Crime Library offers you fascinating accounts of the latest, most sensational crimes that have captured the national attention. St. Martin's is the publisher of John Glatt's riveting and horrifying SECRETS IN THE CELLAR, which shines a light on the man who shocked the world when it was revealed that he had kept his daughter locked in his hidden basement for 24 years. In the Edgar-nominated WRITTEN IN BLOOD, Diane Fanning looks at Michael Petersen, a Marine-turned-novelist found guilty of beating his wife to death and pushing her down the stairs of their home—only to reveal another similar death from his past. In the book you now hold, SLEEP MY DARLINGS, Diane Fanning returns to examine a shocking case of family strife and the death of two children.

St. Martin's True Crime Library gives you the stories behind the headlines. Our authors take you right to the scene of the crime and into the minds of the most notorious murderers to show you what really makes them tick. St. Martin's True Crime Library paperbacks are better than the most terrifying thriller, because it's all true! The next time you want a crackling good read, make sure it's got the St. Martin's True Crime Library logo on the spine—you'll be up all night!

Charles E. Spicer, Jr.
Executive Editor, St. Martin's True Crime Library

Other True Crime Accounts by Diane Fanning

Her Deadly Web

Mommy's Little Girl

A Poisoned Passion

The Pastor's Wife

Out There

Under the Knife

Baby Be Mine

Gone Forever

Through the Window

Into the Water

Written in Blood

From the True Crime Library of
St. Martin's Paperbacks

The Lieutenant Lucinda Pierce mystery series
by Diane Fanning

Wrong Turn

False Front

Twisted Reason

Mistaken Identity

Punish the Deed

The Trophy Exchange

SLEEP MY DARLINGS

Diane Fanning

St. Martin's Paperbacks

SLEEP MY DARLINGS

Copyright © 2013 by Diane Fanning.

For information address St. Martin's Press, 175 Fifth Avenue, New York, NY 10010.

EAN: 978-0-312-94508-4

Printed in the United States of America

St. Martin's Paperbacks edition / May 2013

St. Martin's Paperbacks are published by St. Martin's Press, 175 Fifth Avenue, New York, NY 10010.

10 9 8 7 6 5 4 3 2

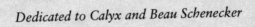

Dedicated to Calyx and Beau Schenecker

CHAPTER 1

On Friday, January 28, 2011, midwesterner Patty Powers, vacationing in Texas, contacted the Tampa Police Department in Florida, concerned about her daughter's well-being. That simple, routine call generated the following message to Officers William Copulos and Gregory Noble: Go to 16305 Royal Park Court in North Tampa: "Check on the welfare of daughter, white female, Julie Schenecker, date of birth one-thirteen-sixty-one. Husband is out of country. She has been depressed, etc. Complaint received. Possible suicidal email from her tonight, now she isn't answering her phone. Also 16 & 13 years of age children are supposed to be home but they are not answering their cell phones either."

The worst the officers thought they'd find was a suicide. They hoped they'd arrive in time to save a life or to uncover a simple, logical explanation. They pulled up to a two-story beige house with white trim at 7:49 on a chilly morning under blue skies. The quiet street in the upscale gated community provided no indication of the horrors they'd discover inside the home.

They walked up a driveway of cement pavers to the garage; Copulos put a hand on either side of his face to block out the sunlight as he peered in the window. He spotted two vehicles parked inside.

Approaching the front of the two-story house, the officers

saw two notes attached to the glass entry door. One read: "No car pool today, went to N Y City." Copulos rang the bell and knocked but received no response. He looked inside and got a view straight through the width of the house all the way back to the rear sliding door. He spotted a one- to two-inch gap between that door and its frame.

The officers circled around to the rear of the home. They entered the backyard through a gate in the six-foot-high wall that enclosed the area. There, in the screened-in area, they saw a white female wearing pajamas and a robe lying next to a cement in-ground swimming pool. Noble shouted, "Tampa Police Department." He got no response.

When they stepped through the screen door, they saw blood on the woman's robe and hands. They called out her name and Julie sat up. She stood and identified herself as Julie Schenecker.

Noble asked, "Are you injured?"

She shook her head and said, "No."

The two officers checked her arms and wrists for injuries but could see no obvious wounds or abrasions. Their concern then shifted to the safety of Calyx and Beau, the two teenagers who lived in the home.

Copulos asked, "Where are your children?"

"They're inside," she said, pointing to the rear door.

"May Officer Copulos and I go into your home and check on the welfare of your kids?"

She agreed and followed the officers into the family room with a beige-tiled floor and yellow-green walls. Once inside, however, she turned belligerent. "What are you doing in my house?" she demanded to know.

Next to the sofa, a small end table was covered with paperwork, including an application to The Hockaday School in Dallas, Texas, mortgage interest statements, and other financial papers. On another table, the officers saw a partially completed Candidate Statement for Groton School in Massachusetts.

The family room led into a formal living room with a love seat, two chairs, a double-doored cabinet, and a stacking end-table grouping. Although it was late January, a decorated Christmas tree stood in the corner, with unopened presents scattered beneath its boughs and on the nearby coffee table, where stockings still hung. Rolls of unused wrapping paper lay on the floor next to one wall.

As Officer Noble approached the doorway of each room, he said, "Tampa Police. Come out with your hands up."

Walking into the unlocked master bedroom on the first floor, he assessed the scene: The bed was unmade. On top of it were pill bottles, a cell phone, a blue spiral notebook, and a flower-topped pen. On the dresser, he saw a Smith & Wesson five-shot revolver. He removed five live rounds and placed them inside the blue cardboard box that held the gun at the time of purchase. He stuck the revolver in his back pocket.

In the master bathroom, he spotted a spa tub, a walk-in shower, and a pile of discarded clothing on the floor. On the six-foot-long vanity, he found an open box of Hornady Critical Defense .38-caliber bullets. Of the twenty-five originally in the box, ten were missing. Next to it were five spent .38-caliber casings.

Along the staircase leading to the second floor, Noble saw eight red-and-white Christmas hats marching up on every other step leading to the top. He passed a Post-it note on the first step. On the third one, he glanced down at a pair of pants, shirts, and socks. On the fourth rise, he saw a Spanish textbook. Up one more step, his eyes scanned paperwork for the PSAT bearing Calyx's name. Nearing the top, he shouted, "Calyx, Beau, are you here? Are you home?"

He approached a desk in an open loft room outside of the bedrooms where a computer chair sat in front of a Gateway laptop. A congealed, blackened pool of blood radiated across the plastic floor protector and onto the white carpet, intermingling with the specks of splatter. Darkened blood covered the seat of the chair, smeared on the armrest and back support, and ran down one of the legs. A single tooth lay on the floor next to the desk. Bloody drag marks led to the closed front bedroom door. The air was thick with the stench of fresh-spilled blood and ominous apprehension. Before opening the door, he warned, "Tampa Police. Come out with your hands up."

Getting no response, he turned the knob and pushed, entering the bedroom of sixteen-year-old Calyx Schenecker. A body, nearly concealed beneath a blanket, stretched out on the bed. He could see a small portion of one hand jutting out from under the covering. Blood stained the sheets and the pillow. He pointed his gun and ordered, "Tampa Police. Show your hands."

The body did not move. Noble pulled back the blanket to reveal a young white female lying on her back, her face covered in blood, a large amount of it around her mouth. Her skin was exceptionally pale. He observed no signs of breathing. He searched for a pulse on her right arm and found nothing. Her body was cold to the touch and as stiff as a plank of wood.

Echoing down the stairway from the second floor, Copulos heard a shout from Noble, "Signal Seven," the Tampa Police code for a dead body. "Possible Signal Five," he added, indicating that it might be a homicide. "Bring Ms. Schenecker to the staircase."

As Copulos escorted Julie to the bottom of the stairs, he heard a knock on the front glass door. He looked over and saw Sergeant John Preyer, who had responded to their call for backup. Holding on to Julie, Copulos walked to the front door and unlocked it. He told the sergeant about the signals. Copulos left Julie with Preyer and went upstairs.

Preyer detected the strong, distinctive odor of alcohol. He wasn't certain if the smell was wafting out of the woman's breath or her clothing. She mumbled incoherently and struggled to remain standing. In his judgment, she appeared impaired by drugs or alcohol or both. He pulled out his handcuffs and attempted to secure Julie, but she stumbled away from him to the sliding glass door. He grabbed her right wrist, bent it back, and pressed her against the door to secure the restraints.

Copulos came back downstairs after viewing the body.

Preyer handed over control of the suspect to Copulos and went upstairs to assist Officer Noble.

Noble backed out of the room with the body and approached the second closed door. "Tampa Police. Come out with your hands up."

After no sound issued from inside the closed room, he eased open the door with Preyer providing cover. After a pause, Noble entered the bedroom of thirteen-year-old Beau Schenecker. The officers saw the normal evidence of the presence of a young boy: a pile of dirty clothing on the floor, a half-empty bottle of Powerade, a small aquarium, soccer trophies, an MP3 Player Station, chewing-gum packs, school supplies, video games, books, and magazines. Nothing was on the bed itself except for a pillow and a blue comforter emblazoned with the Boston Red Sox insignia. The policemen looked in the closet and under the bed.

The room was empty. They had expected to find another body in that room. Could Beau still be alive? Would they discover him hiding somewhere too frightened and confused to respond? Or was another body waiting for them elsewhere in the house—the body of a boy who should have lived a much longer life? Noble and Preyer went downstairs to continue the search for Julie's son.

They entered the garage through the connecting interior door. Next to the door was a chalkboard bearing the message: "2011, Best Year ever." The upbeat normalcy of those words made them cringe.

Inside were two vehicles: a black Volkswagen Passat and a white Honda Odyssey mini-van, with an empty bay between them. The windshield of the Honda had a bullet hole on the passenger's side, leaving behind external beveling and spiderwebbing in the glass. The seat on that side of the mini-van was covered with a white blanket. The side window was covered with blood spatter. Preyer shone a flashlight through the window and saw a human leg sticking out of the covering.

Noble opened the driver's door, reached through, and uncovered the head beneath the blanket. A horrific wound and a massive amount of blood marred the left side of the young boy's face. White fluid foamed around his nose. His seat belt secured him in his upright position. Noble saw no rise and fall in the boy's chest. He searched for a pulse in the boy's left arm and discovered that this body, too, was cold and stiff.

Back inside the home, Preyer led Julie to a sofa. Noble handed her a glass of orange juice. They obtained the dates of birth of her children and the name and birth date of her husband.

Police officers always hope for a happy ending or at least a partial positive outcome when they make a call to check on someone's welfare, but their hopes were dashed in this upscale neighborhood where no one thought it could happen. After taking Julie's statement, they arrested her and led her from her home. Her body twitched; her face contorted; her eyes appeared lost in confusion and despair. She looked more like a terrified, traumatized dog than a human being.

CHAPTER 2

The wreck of a woman who walked out of that upscale Tampa home bore little resemblance to the Julie Schenecker whom many knew, admired, and loved. The image was incongruous with the small-town midwestern girl who excelled academically, physically, and professionally.

Her parents, Jim and Patty Peterson Powers, native Iowans, were married on August 16, 1958, in Chariton, Iowa. Their second child, Julie Kay Powers, was born on January 13, 1961. Exactly one week after her birth, John F. Kennedy took the oath of office as the thirty-fifth president of the United States.

Julie's big brother, David, was two years old when she was born. Two years later, Julie had a sister, Carol. Their father, Jim, worked as an electrical engineer for Shive-Hattery just across the river in Moline, Illinois, and farmed west of Muscatine at their home. Their mother stayed home when her children were young but went on to be a Realtor for more than twenty years and president of the Muscatine Kiwanis Club. The Powerses had three children and eight grandchildren—six of the latter remained living in 2012.

Julie had a comfortable childhood, raised in Muscatine, a town of twenty thousand, filled with lumberjacks and farmers, nestled on bluffs and hills at a major west-south bend in the Mississippi River in Southeast Iowa. The town had been known as Casey's Woodpile, Newburg, and Bloomington before the residents settled on the unique name of Muscatine in 1850.

Lumber was king in the early days as log after log floated down the river to be hauled in when they reached the town, milled to board lumber, doors, and window sashes. Up until the Civil War, Muscatine, a haven for fugitive slaves from the South and freed men from the East, had the largest black population in the state of Iowa. One of these residents, Alexander Clark, was responsible for the desegregation of Iowa public schools in 1868.

Samuel Clemens, better known under his pen name, Mark Twain, lived in the town in the summer of 1855 while working for his brother Orion Clemens at the *Muscatine Journal*. In his book *Life on the Mississippi*, Twain wrote: "And I remember Muscatine—still more pleasantly—for its summer sunsets. I have never seen any, on either side of the ocean, that equaled them. They used the broad smooth river as a canvas and painted on it every imaginable color, from the mottled daintiness and delicacies of the opal, all the way up, through cumulative intensities, to blinding purple and crimson conflagrations which were enchanting to the eye, but sharply tried it at the same time."

In 1887, Muscatine earned its name as the Pearl of the Mississippi when German emigrant John F. Beopple came to town looking for raw materials to create durable buttons. He found machine-punched mussel shells from the river produced buttons that looked like pearls. When production hit its peak in 1905, Muscatine manufactured 1.5 billion buttons, nearly 40 percent of the world's output, and the company employed half of the available workforce in the community.

At the time of Julie's birth, the largest employer in this small farming region was Heinz, followed by Bandag, manufacturers of retread tires, and Hahn Industries, manufacturers of concrete garden statuary. The downtown area was small. The tallest building, a fifteen-story hotel, stood out in the landscape.

Life for teenagers revolved around the high school. To

hang out, the kids went to the one "dinky" mall, Happy Joe's Pizza and Ice Cream Parlor, or Pizza Hut—all fairly typical fare for a rural Midwest community.

Sweet, respectful, and blue-eyed, Julie grew up to be athletic, competitive, and striking. She was always well dressed, her long hair well-kept, and her skin a perpetual tan from her outdoor sports activities.

She and Sylvia Carroll first met in their sophomore algebra class in the brand-new Muscatine High School, situated across the road from an enormous cornfield. They had several classes together over their three years, and both were on the track team: Sylvia as a shot-putter and Julie as a runner.

Julie was one of the stars of that team. She was also a standout on the basketball squad. When she competed, she gave it all she had, wearing purple-and-gold hair ribbons to match her Muskies uniform. As Sylvia Carroll said: "She was the epitome of what wholesome is. You wanted to be like her."

She graduated with about 350 other students in 1978 and went on to the University of Northern Iowa in Cedar Falls to conquer a new challenge.

CHAPTER 3

The University of Northern Iowa (UNI), located on the west side of the Cedar Falls–Waterloo metropolitan area in northeastern Iowa, began in the late 1800s as Iowa State Normal School. After the turn of the century, it became Iowa State Teachers College, then State College of Iowa before being granted university accreditation in 1967.

When Julie arrived on campus in the fall of 1978, the student body had grown to 10,455, far more than half of them were female, and 97 percent of them were from Iowa. The minority population was low enough to be insignificant: just 210 African Americans and only 32 Hispanic students. More than half of the population majored in liberal and vocational arts, and nearly a third planned on becoming teachers after graduation.

It was an institution whose size and prestige had expanded in the previous decade with building projects of particular importance to Julie and all other physical education majors. The new physical education complex was ready for use in the fall of 1971. It housed a unique floor surface installed especially for volleyball. When Julie arrived on campus, she spent many hours there perfecting her skills, mastering the sport, and competing successfully against rivals.

A far more ambitious project, the UNI-Dome, endured cost overruns, project delays, and storm damage before finally hosting its first official event, a wrestling contest between UNI and Iowa, on February 7, 1976. The dome had serious problems with its fabric roof, causing it to deflate twice in the first two years. But by the time Julie matriculated there it had been stabilized. In addition to sporting events, international music stars—such as Foreigner in November 1978 and Mick Jagger in November 1982—performed during her years at the university.

Julie was well liked at UNI, particularly among the others on her volleyball squad. "She had a strong personality but still was a lot of fun to be with," teammate Lisa Pilch said. "When you were with Julie, you were laughing a lot."

Nonetheless, the intensity of her character and competitive spirit often put her at odds with others. She expressed her disapproval in no uncertain terms when she thought a team member was slacking off during a practice. And Julie was as competitive in love as she was in sport. If another woman liked the same guy Julie did, Julie made it clear that she was a rival and that she fully intended to prevail.

Julie's Division I volleyball squad had a stellar season in her senior year. Julie was the team's best middle-hitter and blocker—her skills that year honed to a level of perfection that overwhelmed competing players. UNI was favored to make it to the finals that season. When they approached the regional level of play—the last step on their way to the top—everyone on the team assumed that victory was a foregone conclusion. They didn't count on the flu taking down one of their star players.

Julie succumbed, but her drive to win forced her out onto the court, despite her illness. She gave it her all, but in her weakened state it just wasn't enough. Her below-par performance led her team to snatch defeat from the jaws of victory. The dream of national prominence disintegrated in the face of a microscopic viral organism.

Julie graduated in 1982 with a Bachelor of Arts degree in physical education and coaching, ending her career at UNI with a nagging regret that she had not achieved the championship.

* * *

After graduation, Julie enlisted in the army and was sent to beautiful Monterey off the legendary and scenic Big Sur highway on the Pacific Ocean; with its rugged coast, near-perfect weather, and a wealth of wineries, the area has often been called paradise on earth. It was the perfect setting for an athletic, outdoor-loving person like Julie Powers.

She had not come there, however, to play—the environment was merely a backdrop. Assigned to the Defense Language Institute Foreign Language Center, in the European and Latin American Language School, Julie was tasked with becoming thoroughly proficient in the Russian language and culture.

The roots of the Defense Language Institute stretched back to the days immediately preceding the entry of the United States into World War Two. In November 1941, the army opened a secret school to teach Japanese at the Presidio of San Francisco, in an abandoned airplane hangar at Crissy Field. Four instructors taught sixty students, predominately second-generation Japanese Americans gathered from up and down the West Coast.

Called the Military Intelligence Service Language School, it moved to Camp Savage in Minnesota in 1942, after Japanese Americans along the Pacific Ocean were moved to internment camps. After the war, the school moved to the historic Presidio in Monterey, originally established in 1770, and was renamed the Army Language School.

In 1963, the language studies of all branches of the military were consolidated into the Defense Foreign Language Program, with headquarters in Washington, D.C. The facility in Monterey became the West Coast Branch of that program. In the 1970s, all the scattered facilities merged at that school and it was renamed the Defense Language Institute Foreign Language Center. The school won academic accreditation in 1979.

The total-immersion language instruction provided there condensed the amount of time required to become proficient compared to the traditional classroom model. The mastery of many of the languages could be achieved in as little as twenty-six to thirty-six weeks. However, when Julie arrived there to study Russian she faced a more intensive and lengthier course of instruction—nearly a whole year's worth—because of the need to learn the Cyrillic alphabet in order to become equally skilled in listening, reading, and speaking. The school was committed to producing high-proficiency linguists who become lifelong students of the language and culture.

The school philosophy was based on their belief that this depth of learning cannot occur in a vacuum—a student's comfort with this new form of communication was dependent on an ability to understand the culture, religion, belief and value systems, economic strata, and geopolitical climate of a particular nation. Thus, the curriculum was designed for rapid absorption of the language.

Immersion was the keystone of the program, both in the classroom and in special events such as overnight programs and three-day getaways that placed students in real-life scenarios that required them to use their new language in problem solving. When at the off-site facility, Julie was isolated from everyone who spoke English.

Julie spent those nights in a setting designed like the typical sleeping quarters and kitchens found in the Soviet Union at the time. During the day, she bargained for food and clothing at a marketplace, went through customs, made hotel reservations, and performed other tasks exclusively in Russian.

At the end of her studies in Monterey, Sergeant Julie Powers was an accomplished Russian linguist ready to tackle a real-world assignment with vital implications for national security. The army assigned her to the Eighteenth Military Intelligence Battalion in Munich as a human intelligence collector in 1987.

She was responsible for collecting intelligence for European agencies by interviewing refugees coming from the Eastern Bloc. Her responsibilities included supervising and conducting tactical information gathered through debriefings and interrogations in English and Russian for the National Security Agency. She also screened sources and documents to establish priorities, planned and participated in counterintelligence and force protection operations, translated captured documents and open source publications, and prepared reports and conducted analysis.

Julie did well at the school, but there were three experiences in the military that left a sour taste in her mouth: standing still as a tape measure was used to take her body measurements, undergoing the white-glove inspections of her barracks rooms, and having to provide a urinalysis sample in front of female senior officers. All three seemed so invasive and bore a high potential for embarrassment.

Julie took satisfaction in winning one battle against the system of regulation and obedience. It centered on her pink Cannondale bicycle, an innovative high-performance touring bike with an oversized aluminum frame and fat-tubed look that made its light weight surprising. Priced far higher than a typical amateur bicycle, it was one of Julie's treasured possessions. She always brought it inside and parked it in her living room.

One time, during inspection, a sergeant told her that a bike sitting inside was not acceptable. The sergeant with him came to Julie's defense, saying, "That bike is worth more than your car, Sergeant." Julie was allowed to keep it inside.

Other downsides of her work in the office included her loathing of the electric typewriters she had to use and having a co-worker whose paper cuts always seemed to be bleeding all over her carbon-copy reports. Outdoors, Julie frequently cursed the cobblestones paving McGraw Street that trashed the heels of her pumps.

She had a lot of upsides to her posting, too. She really loved the work and living in Bavarian Germany. Bavaria was one of the oldest states of Europe and the largest state in contemporary Germany, covering 20 percent of that nation's landmass. The area has always been steeped in traditions different from those in the rest of the country—even their religion was different. The majority of Bavarians were Catholic while most Germans were Lutheran. And the Bavarian fondness for their distinctive regional food and drink is legendary.

One of Julie's favorite Bavarian experiences was the fun and camaraderie of the Starkbierfest, or Strong Beer Festival, an annual three-week-long celebration of stout drinking that takes place during Lent. Most of the time, Christian religious observances called for decorum and abstinence at that time of year. Not in Munich—not during Lent, at least not since 1773. In that year, Brother Barnabas, a monk at the Paulaner monastery in Munich, wanted to ease the deprivation the brotherhood endured with fasting and refraining from solid food during that religious season. Although eating was forbidden, drinking was not, so he created the perfect solution. He brewed a batch of strong beer—a process that used less water and left more grain in the beverage— and named it Salvator. One liter contained the equivalent amount of grain a person would get by eating sixteen loaves of bread. His brothers loved it, but they worried if it might be too good to be acceptable.

To decide this issue, they loaded up the beer to make the trek to the Vatican to get the pope's opinion on its acceptability. The barrels bounced around on a horse-drawn flatbed, crossing southern Germany, scaling the Alps, and descending into the alpine valleys. Along the way, the altitude and extreme temperature variances impacted the beverage. They crossed Austria and entered Italy, where temperatures got rather high.

Even after they arrived in Rome, the beer had to sit and wait for weeks until the pope would grant them an audience. When Brother Barnabas went before His Eminence, he explained the concern that drinking his beer would not show the proper penitence required of the devout during Lent.

The pope felt a taste test was in order. What he drank no longer had a taste that bore any resemblance to the strong beer's original flavor. The pope found the beer stressed by the traveling conditions and temperature and elevation changes vile and undrinkable. He said that if the Munich monks could drink that foul brew they were obviously the most penitent men in all of Christendom.

Originally, the monks were forbidden from serving Salvator to anyone outside of their brotherhood. The rule, however, was repealed in 1780, because the monks never really followed it and the demand from Bavarians on the outside could not be ignored.

With a recipe unchanged for more than two hundred years, the Paulaner Salvator has remained the most well-known of the *Starkbiers* out of Munich. However, others have eagerly jumped into the strong beer market, creating their own versions of the brew with names such as Triumphator, Maximator, Aviator, Scapegoat, Celebrator, and many more. The Starkbierfest has always overflowed with a diverse variety of taste sensations from the different breweries that participated.

Since these special brews were born in Germany, a country known for its obsession with rules and regulations, strict standards were written into law, dictating minimum percentages of "wort," the grain solids dissolved in each liter. The beverage was divided into two categories: Bockbier, requiring at least 16 percent wort, and Doppelbock, which needed no less than 18 percent. Bavarian Catholics gladly gave up bread for Lent in exchange for more *Starkbier*.

When Julie went to her first festival, she absorbed the culture trappings and mimicked the actions of the Germans around her. A woman, beautifully attired in a traditional dirndl, arrived at the table with a handful of cool ceramic steins, foam running down their sides. She placed a liter in front of each person at the table, many of the women dressed in dirndls and men wearing lederhosen.

Mugs raised in unison, hearty voices shouted, "Prost." Steins clinked and gulps went down throats. Together the containers smacked back down on the table, making it shake. Men wiped the froth from their mouths with the back of their hands and laughter lasted all night long.

As if the sustenance of that hearty beer was not filling

enough, the festival abounded in traditional Bavarian food: thick, soft, chewy pretzels with a crispy, salty outer crust paired with a fondue made of cheese and strong beer for dipping; *Schweinshaxe,* a pig knuckle with a crunchy outer skin; thick hunks of regional cheeses, German potato salad; and corned-beef and sauerkraut sandwiches on rye bread, drowning in melted Swiss.

At her first festival, Julie learned how the short, sober walk from the base to the beer hall transformed into a long, arduous trudge after the consumption of stein after stein of the 8.1 percent brew. Nonetheless, she went back year after year—the torturous walk home was an acceptable price of a night of unabashed fun.

Another high point for Julie in Bavaria was organizing and coaching a volleyball team of officers. She approached the responsibility with energetic enthusiasm.

K. C. Dreller, an intelligence officer who worked with her, said: "She was supergood at it. I imagine she was supergood at everything she did. Anybody that was in that field was a type A personality." He added that Julie "had a type A personality, but everybody I worked with was one because of the nature of our business."

It was during her time coaching the men's volleyball team that Julie's path first crossed that of rising army officer Parker Schenecker.

CHAPTER 4

Edmund Morris "Eddie" Schenecker was Fort Worth, Texas, born and bred, arriving in the city on June 6, 1933. He made a halfhearted, peripatetic attempt at higher education, attending both Oberlin College, in northeastern Ohio, and Miami of Ohio University (now known simply as Miami University) in southwestern Ohio near Cincinnati. When the Korean War commenced, he escaped the books by joining the army. When his tour of duty was completed, he resumed his education, attending Texas Christian University (TCU) right in his hometown of Fort Worth.

In the late 1950s he developed a passion for New Orleans, where he met his future wife, debutante Nancy Trousdale of Monroe, Louisiana. He frequently said, "I reside in Fort Worth, but I live in New Orleans." Nonetheless, Eddie and Nancy settled down in Fort Worth, Texas, to raise their family. Their first child, Edmund, was born on January 11, 1961. Their second son, Parker, arrived nineteen months later on November 17, 1962.

During World War Two, Fort Worth exploded with growth as a manufacturing center for airplane, helicopter, and other military products. Four years after that conflict ended, an epic flood tore through the city—horses were seen on roofs, eleven people lost their lives, and property damage exceeded $11 million.

The Army Corps of Engineers came to the area, determined to prevent a repeat of the disaster by channelizing the Trinity River and building a sturdy levee system to protect the city from devastation. That improvement heralded a population expansion. By the time the Schenecker boys arrived on the scene, there were more than 350,000 residents in the once rustic town mostly known only for the historic Chisholm Trail feeder routes in the state that merged at the stockyards for the drive north.

Fort Worth was a footnote in an American tragedy when Parker was just one year old. President John Fitzgerald Kennedy checked into the venerable Hotel Texas in the downtown area on Thursday, November 21, 1963. His charismatic personality filled the air over the city with hope, optimism, and faith in the future. No one suspected how little future remained for JFK.

The next morning, under rainy skies, the president addressed an impromptu gathering of two thousand local residents in the hotel parking lot. "There are no faint hearts in Fort Worth," he told the cheering crowd, and continued to praise the city for its role in the security of the nation. "Fort Worth, as it did in World War Two, as it did in developing the best bomber system in the world, the B-Fifty-Eight, and as it will now do in developing the best fighter system in the world, the TFX, Fort Worth will play its proper part. . . . Here in this rain in Fort Worth, we are moving forward."

At the conclusion of his remarks, Kennedy walked around the barricades into a crowd of outstretched hands, shaking as many as he could to the delight of those who expected nothing more than a glimpse of their president. He went back into the hotel to the restaurant where he was the scheduled speaker at a Chamber of Commerce breakfast.

From there, Kennedy traveled by motorcade to Carswell Air Force Base, northwest of downtown, where he boarded *Air Force One* for the short flight to Love Field in the neighboring city of Dallas. The ten-mile meandering drive wandered through suburban developments and traveled the traditional parade route in the downtown area on its way to the luncheon at the Dallas Trade Mart. Crowds of people lined the presidential route.

The celebratory atmosphere was shattered in one moment when everything went wrong as the motorcade turned into Dealey Plaza on the way to the entrance ramp onto Stemmons Freeway. Shots rang out from the sixth floor of the Texas School Book Depository, a seven-story building that provided storage for school textbooks and related materials as well as housing a business that fulfilled orders for all these supplies. The front windows of the structure overlooked the plaza on the western end of the downtown area.

The open convertible, carrying the president, the First Lady, Texas governor John Connally, and his wife, Nellie, was the target of the gunfire. The first shot hit John Kennedy in his upper back, nicking the knot on his tie as it exited his body. The bullet then continued on, hitting the governor in the chest, before lodging in the inner thigh of his left leg.

It remained a matter of debate whether one or two additional shots were fired before the final shot ripped through the president's skull, causing Jackie Kennedy to scream, "They have killed my husband! I have his brains in my hands!"

The car accelerated, racing toward the Parkland Memorial Hospital. The president was declared dead after his arrival. The governor survived his injuries, despite their life-threatening nature.

Kennedy's assassination rocked Fort Worth, particularly those who had listened to him in the rain or sat in the dry comfort of the hotel dining room. Hours before, Kennedy was alive, vibrant, and close enough to touch, right there in their town. Nancy and Eddie expected that night's news to be dominated by footage of his local speeches. Instead, their city's bright moment was overshadowed by the dark news from neighboring Dallas. The presidential assassination wrapped the nation in a blanket of inconsolable grief. The Scheneckers, like nearly everyone in Fort Worth, Dallas, and the whole state of Texas, carried the additional burden of shared shame and guilt.

* * *

Despite Fort Worth's prominence in the defense industry during Parker's early years, it remained a sleepy town. Local history buff Jim Nichols said, "The downtown area was so quiet at night, you could fire cannons down the streets and hit nothing but grackles"—the large, raucous black birds that are ubiquitous in Texas.

Still, despite its exploding population, the city maintained a small-town, family-friendly environment with a western cultural flair. The good school system, the high employment rate, and its low-key approach to politics made Fort Worth an appealing place to live.

Rivalry with their next-door neighbor, the more cosmopolitan Dallas, pushed Fort Worth forward. In 1965, before either of the Schenecker boys started school, the city approved a record-breaking $33.9 million bond issue to fund new park and recreation facilities, street repairs, a new city hall and police building, and other needed improvements.

As the Schenecker boys grew up, their hometown was transformed into an exuberant city while maintaining its strong can-do attitude, small-town flavor, and distinct cowboy flair. Trinity Park and Forest Park created havens for family recreation. The Fort Worth Zoo, opened in 1909 with nothing more than one lion, two bear cubs, an alligator, a coyote, a peacock, and a few rabbits, had expanded with many more animals, including monkeys, sea lions, and reptiles in herpetarium. The stock show and rodeo moved from the stockyard to the Will Rogers Memorial Center's domed coliseum, the first structure of its kind in the world in 1944, making the event the first indoor rodeo venue in the country. Broadening the cultural opportunities were the museums in the city. The Fort Worth Children's Museum, which became the Fort Worth Museum of Science and History when Parker was six years old, housed the Noble Planetarium (named after Charlie Mary Noble), a delightful experience for any child. When Parker turned ten, the respected Kimball Art Museum opened its doors. Rounding out the city's offerings was the Fort Worth Art-Museum Center (now known as the Modern

Art Museum of Fort Worth), the oldest art museum in the state of Texas, chartered seventy years before Parker's birth.

The impetus for the expansion of the city was the opening of the Dallas/Fort Worth International Airport in 1972. It stimulated the arrival of many corporate entities at Fort Worth, including American Airlines.

Downtown during Parker's teenage years was transformed into a bustling city center. The Tandy Corporation, the RadioShack company, built two tall office towers with an ice rink between the two buildings. The Bass family built the first hotel constructed downtown since World War One, added two forty-story office buildings, and developed Sundance Square. The Woodbine corporation bought the Hotel Texas, where Kennedy spoke on the last day of his life, gutted it, and renovated it, creating a fresh, vital showcase for tourists and visitors to the city.

Parker's home life wasn't as consistently upbeat as his surroundings. His father's alcoholism created a fragile atmosphere for the family where unpredictability was the norm.

Some blemishes existed beneath the surface of his hometown, too, subverting the sense of harmony in the community in the early sixties. Although race relations in Fort Worth were far more civil than in neighboring Dallas, problems still arose when school integration became the law of the land. Two college preparatory schools were created from this conflict: Fort Worth Country Day School and Trinity Valley School. From the start, their high academic standards attracted children from economically advantaged families, but the birth of these schools was clearly instigated by a desire to avoid the presence of minorities in the public schools.

Parker and his brother both attended Fort Worth Country Day School more than a decade after its formation, at a time when the racist origins had already faded away in public memory.

By the time Eddie gave up drinking and joined the North 40 chapter of Alcoholics Anonymous, the negative impact of his behavior had already imprinted on the character of his sons. Eddie rebuilt his life, becoming active in the Steeplechase Club and the River Crest Country Club in Fort Worth and the Boston Club, a gentlemen's club since 1840, and Lake Shore Club in New Orleans. He also served as "The Grand Claw" of the Athenian Literary and Crustacean Society.

Parker, his childhood marked by his father's erratic behavior, appeared determined not to follow his father's example. He charted a path in an entirely different direction.

CHAPTER 5

Fort Worth Country Day School was growing physically as well in reputation while the Schenecker brothers were in attendance—from the time Edmund enrolled until Parker graduated, there was constantly at least one major building or annex project under way. Parker performed well academically and excelled on the track team as a hurdler. He graduated in the Class of 1980.

In his senior year, Parker selected Washington and Lee University in Lexington, Virginia, to be his institution of higher education. He enrolled in the ROTC program, adding another layer of responsibility to his course studies.

The venerable liberal arts undergraduate school was steeped in history and tradition. It was named Washington College in honor of General and President George Washington after he gave its first major endowment in 1796, literally saving the school from collapse. In 1865, the Board of Trustees unanimously elected General Robert E. Lee as president of their college. He was flattered as he considered the job offer but had some trepidation about accepting it. He was concerned that his leadership of the Confederate army "might draw upon the College a feeling of hostility. I think it the duty of every citizen in the present condition of the Country, to do all in his power to aid in the restoration of peace and harmony." The board eagerly awaited his decision. To their delight, he delivered it in person, riding into town on his horse Traveler to accept the position.

Within days of Lee's death in 1870, the trustees voted to change the name of the school to Washington and Lee University. Lee's contribution to the culture of the school went far beyond the name, though. Numerous changes occurred under his watch. The Lexington Law School was incorporated into the college; construction of the chapel that would bear his name got under way; the traditional curriculum of uniform studies for all was abandoned in favor of a departmental system where students could elect their own course of study; and the first journalism instruction at any college in the world was established under his leadership.

These changes made a significant impact on the culture of the campus, but they paled in comparison to the single most influential contribution he made to the university—one that no one else had matched before or since. He established Washington and Lee's signature honor system when he said, "We have but one rule here and it is that every student must be a gentleman." With those words, honor became the moral cornerstone of the school. The Virginia Military Institute and the University of Virginia had honor systems, too, but they had codified theirs with a long list of regulations regarding behavior and a multiplicity of possible punishments.

At Washington and Lee, their code called upon the student body to determine the definition of an honor violation and to administer the one punishment they could impose on violators: expulsion. Lee's system created an atmosphere of trust at the school. Professors accepted a student's word without question, assuming that they all took their incoming vow to act honorably in all academic and nonacademic endeavors to heart.

Because of this environment, most exams were self-scheduled. Professors frequently assigned take-home, closed-book finals with an explicit trust that the students were being honest when they pledged that they had not received any unacknowledged aid. Parker gained a strong basis of ideals to guide him through his professional and personal life in his years at Washington and Lee.

That was not all Parker took from the experience. The school's yearbook was called *The Calyx*, the name of a collection of sepals in a flower, symbolizing "sweetness and loveliness." He'd remember this title years later when it was time to decide on a name for his oldest child.

When Parker entered the university in the fall of 1980, the student body surpassed sixteen hundred members. The sitting university president, Robert E. R. Huntley, was the only alumnus in the twentieth century inaugurated to this position. During his service prior to Parker's arrival, the first African Americans graduated from Washington and Lee and the first women were admitted to the School of Law. The undergraduate body remained male only until the year after Parker moved away from Lexington.

Classmate Eric Storey said Washington and Lee "is a small school and everyone knows everyone else. Everyone was Parker's friend. He was the true gentleman that we all aspired to be. He kept real balance in his life."

In demonstration of the latter, Parker complemented his diligence in academic studies by playing linebacker on the football team. But his final year was marred by tragedy. On April 11, the Phi Gamma Delta House at Preston Street and Jackson Avenue caught on fire. One student died in the blaze. The death had a strong impact on everyone in the school, including Parker. Reminders of mortality sat uneasy on the minds of anyone that young.

Less than two months later, the Class of 1984 bid farewell to the campus. Parker graduated cum laude with a degree in French and as a Distinguished Military Graduate. For his work in ROTC he also received the Military Order of the World Wars award and was commissioned as a second lieutenant in army intelligence.

CHAPTER 6

After graduating from W and L, Parker went into the army's Officer Training Program at Fort Huachuca, the prestigious Arizona facility that serves as the army's intelligence center and the Eleventh Military Intelligence Brigade. The base bore historical significance because it was the unit charged with protecting the Mexican border from the threat of the Chiricahua Apaches led by Geronimo from 1858 to 1886. It was also the headquarters for the Tenth Calvary Regiment, the only African-American unit under American command that fought the Germans during World War One.

The fort abutted the town of Sierra Vista, Arizona, in Cochise County, near Tombstone and just five miles north of the Mexican border. It was an area of stark natural beauty featuring mountains, desert, and, surprisingly, a spot of wetlands. The closest city of any size was Tucson—an hour and a half away.

Sierra Vista was known as the Hummingbird Capital of the United States because of the fourteen species of the tiny, captivating bird living in the nearby Ramsey Canyon. At an elevation of 4,625 feet, it had nearly ideal weather with an average high of seventy-five degrees and an average low of fifty.

From there, First Lieutenant Parker Schenecker reported to duty in Munich, Germany, in 1986, as the aide to Army and Air Force Exchange Service Commander Brigadier General E. B. Leedy. Schenecker was serving in this position when he met Sergeant Julie Powers.

Munich was the heart of Bavarian Germany and the birthplace of the Nazi Party. The city was 70 percent destroyed during World War Two, but by the time international athletes and the press arrived there for the 1972 Summer Olympics the restoration was complete, with special attention given to restoring historic areas and modernizing infrastructure.

That prominent event earned the city another historical black eye. The 1972 Munich Olympic Games were in their second week of exuberant competition on September 5. At 4:30 that morning while the athletes slept, eight members of the terrorist group Black September scaled a high chain-link fence around the Olympic Village and stole keys to rooms occupied by participants from Israel.

The terrorists, wearing track suits and carrying duffel bags packed with assault rifles, pistols, and grenades, burst into the rooms, killing a coach and a weight lifter and taking nine others hostage. They demanded safe passage to Egypt for 234 prisoners—predominately Palestinians—detained in Israeli jails as well as the founders of the Red Army Faction held in German penitentiaries.

After negotiations provided transportation to an airfield, a rescue attempt planned there failed. As a result, all remaining nine Israeli coaches and athletes, a West German police officer, and five of the eight members of Black September were shot dead.

Bavaria, however, had more to offer than dark notes in history. It is surrounded by the great natural beauty of mountains and gorges with waterfalls; stunning palaces and romantic castles; a Benedictine monastery with the area's most loved beer gardens; and an unparalleled calendar of festivals from the world-renowned Oktoberfest in the fall to the Strong Beer Festival in the spring. It is a land of lederhosen, dirndls, and lots and lots of beer.

* * *

While stationed in Munich, Parker was responsible for the bidirectional flow of information between the commander and his subordinate military units and managed family support programs and human resources efficiency. Love was in the air when volleyball brought Julie and Parker together in 1987. Julie was the coach of the men's team, and when Parker signed up to participate it brought him into Julie's orbit.

Sharing common interests and goals, they were drawn to each other and began to date. Parker told *People:* "The more time we spent around each other, the more we fell in love."

For the young army officer and the enlisted translator who specialized in Russian, the posting in Germany was a chance to launch great careers. In the late 1980s, the Cold War was still going strong. The Berlin Wall still divided Germany, the teetering Soviet Union was still a powerful adversary, and the U.S. military intelligence operations were focused in West Germany.

Parker remained in Munich but was transferred to the Sixty-Sixth Military Intelligence, a group whose primary mission was to conduct counterintelligence operations. He served as commander of the HHC (Headquarters and Headquarters Company), a military unit by definition and practice that ranged in size from 85 to 225 soldiers, under Executive Officer Greg Zellmer.

Parker developed and managed training and life support programs for headquarters personnel; provided food service, billeting, supply, and maintenance support; and shouldered the responsibility for internal morale and discipline programs for the theater troops.

Timothy G. Fredrickson, a former army Slavic linguist who served with Julie and Parker, described their unit as "a group of the elite of the elite." The unit, located in a Cold War hot spot where defectors and other personnel assets were abundant, "was the only place in the entire U.S. Army an interrogator could do his job on a daily basis."

Paul Muehlmann, a retired army intelligence officer who served with Parker and Julie during this period of time, said, "We played volleyball together for the Munich military team and I have very fond memories of both of them. Parker was an outstanding young officer."

CHAPTER 7

In 1990, the army sent Parker back to Fort Huachuca as an instructor and the executive officer of his brigade. His relationship with Julie survived the separation. The time apart was not easy for Julie. She was diagnosed with depression in 1992 and treated with medication by a psychiatrist. Even after Parker's return to Munich, she did not inform him of this illness. She saved her secret until after they were married.

Julie and Parker grew their relationship until it was time to make a deeper commitment. When they were ready to take the next step, the Schenecker and Powers families gathered together in New Orleans, on October 10, 1992, at the historic 140-year-old Trinity Episcopal Church on the corner of Jackson and Plaquemines Streets, at the nexus of the Uptown and Garden Districts. Trinity is one of the more noteworthy houses of worship in New Orleans, and its ornate Gothic/Norman splendor with breathtaking architectural detail welcomes attendees into the interior, where vaulted ceilings added a formality and sense of permanence to the exchange of vows. As fading light drifted through elaborate stained-glass windows, Parker and Julie were wed in a six o'clock service. Afterwards, the new couple celebrated with guests at the New Orleans Country Club, best known for its Robert Weed–designed golf course.

The newlyweds returned to Bavaria and the Rose Barracks in the town of Vilseck. In 1994, Julie decided to leave the army and become a stay-at-home mom. The Scheneckers' first child was born on September 12, 1994, in a hospital located in nearby Sulzbach-Rosenberg. They named her Calyx Powers—the first name a sentimental salute to Parker's influential years at Washington and Lee University and the second a tribute to the baby's maternal heritage.

After a stint at Leighton Barracks at Würzburg, in the northern tip of Bavaria, the new family transferred stateside to Fort Leavenworth in Kansas, the oldest continually operating military installation west of the Mississippi River. It sat beside Leavenworth, the first city incorporated in the state of Kansas, on the west bank of the Missouri River in the Dissected Till Plains region of the North American lowlands. Past glaciations had left behind a region of rolling hills and rich, fertile soil, sitting on the edge of the Corn Belt.

At the outbreak of the Civil War, Camp Lincoln was established there to train Kansas volunteers, and its use as a training and education facility continued from there. The garrison occupied fifty-six hundred acres of land, covered with one thousand buildings and fifteen hundred base housing quarters.

The base was home to the United States Disciplinary Barracks, the only maximum-security prison for military personnel of all branches of service, and a low-security prison under the command of the army; a base hospital; an airfield; the Fort Leavenworth National Cemetery; headquarters for a National Guard mechanized infantry division, Battle Command Training Center, main facility for training and development of brigade staff in the National Guard; the U.S. Army Training and Document Command (TRADOC) Analysis Center; the Foreign Military Studies Office; and the U.S. Army's Combined Arms Center, often called the intellectual center of the army. The latter operated the Command and General Staff School, which all modern five-star army generals, including George Marshall, Douglas MacArthur, Dwight Eisenhower, Hap Arnold, and Omar Bradley, have attended.

Parker was now stationed there to undergo Intermediate Level education, a ten-month graduate-level program with a curriculum that included leadership philosophy, military history, military planning, and decision-making processes. The goal of the institution was to prepare field-grade officers to lead and command organizations. Parker was clearly designated as an officer on the rise.

The Scheneckers settled into Lansing, with its nine thousand residents the second most populous city in Leavenworth County. Lansing was home to the Lansing Correctional Facility, where notorious killers of the Clutter family, Perry Smith and Richard Hickok—forever remembered in the Truman Capote classic *In Cold Blood*—were hanged in 1965. This facility remained the largest employer in Lansing.

Parker, Julie, and Calyx moved into a neat, pretty white house at the end of the cul-de-sac on Fourth Street. Calyx met her first best friend here, Kassie Krivo. Kassie lived a short distance up the road and around the corner on Debra Street.

Julie and Karen Krivo were mothers in the same playgroup, bringing the two little toddlers together on a regular basis. For Kassie's second birthday party in the fall of 1996, she and Calyx dressed up as princesses—clad in pink from head to toe.

But the friendship was cut short in June of 1997 and she had to bid farewell to her best friend when Kassie's family moved away, giving Calyx her first experience with a loss that has always been a regular ordeal for children in military families. Calyx wrapped her arms around Kassie's neck and gave her the biggest good-bye squeeze her tiny arms could muster.

The family's stay stateside didn't last long. In no time, they were transferred once again. The Scheneckers packed their bags and journeyed to a far more exotic posting in Hawaii.

CHAPTER 8

The new home for the three Scheneckers was on the island of Oahu, the third-largest Hawaiian island, where the majority of the state's diverse population resides. It was the seat of the government since the unification of the islands in 1810 and remained that way after Hawaii achieved statehood in 1959. It is a large island but still manageable for exploration—it just takes an hour to drive from Honolulu in the southern tip to the wild Pacific coast in the north.

The weather there whispers "paradise" on every breeze, all year round. During the winter, from November through April, temperatures range from the low seventies to the mid-eighties. During the only other season, summer, seventy-four- to eighty-eight-degree readings are the norm. Even though the average humidity is a fairly consistent 53 percent, gentle trade winds keep even the warmest days pleasant and comfortable.

The island played an important role in American history as the site of a day of infamy. On the morning of December 7, 1941, the Imperial Japanese Navy launched an attack on Oahu's Pearl Harbor, putting its name on the tip of every American's tongue and pushing the country into World War Two. The attack damaged or destroyed warships and aircraft, caused the deaths of more than twenty-four hundred

American servicemen and nearly six dozen civilians, and scarred any sense of security in the far-flung island chain.

Parker was stationed at Schofield Barracks at the foot of the Waianae Mountain Range in Central Oahu, separated from the town of Wahiaw by Lake Wilson. Schofield had been established in 1908 to provide mobile defense of Pearl Harbor and the surrounding area. The Dole Plantation, with its world-class shrub maze, and the Hawaii Plantation Village, reenacting Oahu's past, were near the base, as was the Aloha Stadium, the venue for the University of Hawaii football games and the arena for the annual NFL Pro Bowl.

With dramatic mountains, a placid lake, and the roaring ocean at her fingertips, outdoorsy Julie was in her element. In addition to the multitude of physical activities, the cultural and artistic events and locales never left her at a loss for what to do around the island.

Schofield Barracks was a hive of activity, too. When the Scheneckers arrived, the population of the base exceeded fourteen thousand. Their home base itself bore a whiff of romance, as it was the principal setting for James Jones' best-selling novel and blockbuster movie, *From Here to Eternity,* featuring the immortal love scene on the beach between Deborah Kerr and Burt Lancaster. Since the cost of housing is extraordinarily high in Hawaii, most families lived on the base. Officers housing was to the north side of the area off Wilikina Drive, inside the gate, a block down Leilehua Avenue, a third of the way down Baldwin Road. The biggest bulk of the installation's 2.8 square miles of acreage on the base was Area X, a huge training area where assault operations could be staged and firing ranges abounded.

On September 29, 1997, the Schenecker clan grew by one more member with the birth of Powers Beau Schenecker at Tripler Army Medical Center in Honolulu, the state capital and jumping-off point for visitors to the nearby world-renowned Waikiki Beach.

On the surface, Julie, now the mom of two, seemed to

have found real contentment in paradise. In actuality, Julie suffered significant postpartum depression after her son's birth and went back on medications. Parker told *People* "Julie was a fantastic mother early on when the kids were needing nursing and nurturing. They gave her a lot of joy. It gave me a lot of joy watching her with the kids." He said that with the knowledge that except for the period of time when she was pregnant Julie relied on antidepressants to maintain her stability.

In less than two weeks after the birth of his son, Parker's maternal grandmother, Louisette Billeaud Trousdale, died in the St. Anna's Residence in New Orleans at the age of ninety-three. The family bid her farewell at a graveside service in the Review Cemetery in Monroe, Louisiana. Parker was one of seven grandchildren to mourn her passing.

The next year, Parker lost a parent when his father died, at the age of sixty-five, after a lengthy illness, on Sunday, July 12, 1998. After a private family funeral, a memorial service was held exactly a week later at Parker's alma mater, Fort Worth Country Day School. In lieu of flowers, the family requested that donations be made to the Edmund Morris Schenecker Scholarship Fund at that school or to Alcoholics Anonymous.

The year 1999 was a miserable one for Darcelle, a woman who would soon play a significant role in the lives of the Schenecker family, on the island of Oahu. On Mother's Day, in May 1999, she and her visiting sister made a trip to Sacred Falls State Park, named for the spectacular eighty-foot waterfall that lay at the end of a small canyon in the Kaluanui Gulch. Located not too far, geographically, from Schofield Barracks, direct access is blocked by the rugged Mililani Mauka Launani Valley and the Ewa Forest Reserve. Getting there required taking the Kamehameha Highway, a coastal route that looped around the northern tip of Oahu.

A hike into the park was an adventurous trip—lives had been lost in the past because of flash floods and stumbles on the slippery rocks encountered on the journey to the top. No one, however, anticipated the deadly event that occurred that day.

Without warning, boulders and rocks collapsed, sending the debris tumbling onto the people in the valley below. Eight lives were lost and fifty people were injured. Darcelle survived, but her vacationing sister was counted among the dead. The park was closed indefinitely after that fatal rock-fall, and the public still remain barred from it thirteen years later.

To compound her grief, Darcelle's boyfriend left her. She was alone, lonely, and feeling quite abandoned. She was living in a three-bedroom home in Waialua that she'd bought when she turned forty. Now even the beauty of her environment could not lift the pall of depression that hung over her days. The home suddenly seemed too large for just one resident—its emptiness mocked her sorrow and sense of estrangement.

She posted availability ads seeking a roommate, hoping to find someone willing to watch over her pets when she traveled away from home. At that same time, Parker Schenecker was called back to the East Coast, but he and Julie did not want to move the kids during the cold of winter back in the continental United States. Julie decided to stay with them in Hawaii for another six months. To do that, she needed off-base housing.

Julie responded to Darcelle's ad, driving north through pineapple fields on her way to the coast and the other woman's beach house. At that time, the once bustling, booming town of Waialua, the home of what the natives called the world's best sugar, was staggering under the economic upheaval that was caused in October 1996 when the Waialua Sugar Mill, the last sugar plantation on the island of Oahu, stopped production after more than one hundred years in operation. At the time, that facility, a subsidiary of the Dole Corporation, was producing 8 percent of all the sugar in the island chain. The smokestack of the old mill still dominated the skyline. In time, the sugar mill would be retrofitted to produce coffee and chocolate, but when Julie arrived there was no activity in the plant itself. Despite the abandoned mill, the natural beauty of the North Shore region was spectacular, dwarfing any downside. Waialua was located near Haleiwa, the historic surf town with a laid-back ambience. Situated on seven miles of thick sandy beaches, Waialua was a ringside seat for much that drew visitors to the upper reaches of the island.

That stretch of beach was home to the storied Banzai Pipeline. The big, glassy waves so close to perfection made it a surfer's Mecca, drawing the best in the world. These massive waves often swell up to thirty feet or more, posing dangers for even the most experienced practitioners of the sport. Yet still they came to worship at the altar of the power of the Pacific Ocean, risking wipeout and even death, as they strove to conquer that power, at least for a brief, glorious moment that would be a highlight of their lives. The exhilarating high of a successful ride created an addiction that pulled them back to the risk again and again.

During the winter months, the area hosted premiere surfing events, including the Super Bowl of wave riding, the Vans Triple Crown of Surfing. During the summer months, though, the waves subsided to manageable heights, creating a far more tranquil environment for swimming, sunbathing, and family outings.

When Darcelle learned that Julie had two small children, she balked at first. Her sister had died violently, and Darcelle just wanted a simple, peaceful life. She couldn't imagine having that with children in her home.

But the tall blonde who walked into Darcelle's home was hard to resist. Julie loved the house and its location. She pointed to the nice yard where her children could play. She pleaded with Darcelle to give her family a chance for the six months remaining before they joined her husband back east.

Darcelle relented and the three moved in to share her home and she never regretted the decision. The kids were great. Calyx was a sweet old soul at five years old, always questioning things, forever wanting to learn more. She loved to play in the garden of the beach house, reveling in the abundance and lushness of the tropical flowers—her favorites were the spider lilies. She was a darling little girl with a very cute face. The placement of the freckles on her cheeks and across her nose appeared to have been designed by an artist rather than the haphazard whim of genetics.

Two-year-old Beau was all boy, with a mop of blond hair and the deepest dimples. "A little cup of poi and full of sweetness," Darcelle said. The little toddler lifted her spirits in a dark time. He loved to start the day by throwing his toys down the stairs to awaken the household. He often did crazy little things, bending over and making faces, anything to make Darcelle laugh.

One morning, Beau had an attack of conscience when he realized his boisterousness had gotten out of control. He slipped into Darcelle's room, placed a Pepsi on her nightstand, and whispered, "I'm sorry."

Julie struck Darcelle as a normal, decent mom who approached parenting with a lot of creativity. She was very organized, keeping the kids busy with a nonstop cycle of activities. The three of them loved to drive around the island with the convertible top down, relishing the sun on their faces.

Julie constantly made checklists of to-do items that she followed without fail. She played volleyball with another tall, beautiful, athletic woman, a financial reporter named Karen. With Darcelle, though, Julie was a closed book. Most of their conversations were just surface interactions; only once or twice in the six months they lived together did Julie open up about anything and really talk in depth.

Julie was definitely not an intimidated little military wife. She was determined to take care of things on her own. Overall, Julie was upbeat and very good with her children; Darcelle saw no shadows of the darkness that would fall with sudden finality in the years to come.

CHAPTER 9

In the summer of 1999, Julie and the children joined Parker stateside. First the family moved to Woodbridge, Virginia, and then on to Columbia, Maryland. As a military family, they moved a lot. Jack Armstrong, who knew Parker in high school, told *People* that keeping a military family intact comes with increasing upheavals, fear, and great expectations. "To live in that uncertainty year after year really takes a toll."

It was not easy for Julie or any military wife. Many felt she gave up a promising career and military dreams to support a family while Parker continued his military aspirations and was often deployed overseas. Living vicariously, instead of directly following her own dreams, did not seem to work well for her.

In 2001, Julie suffered a severe and debilitating episode of depression for which she was hospitalized at a National Institutes of Health facility. While there she was diagnosed with severe depression; bipolar disorder, a condition where a sufferer's moods swung from a very good or irritable mood to a lethargic depression; and schizoaffective disorder, a condition that caused a loss of contact with reality, or a state of psychosis, as well as mood problems. She received nine months of intensive inpatient treatment. In her absence from home, Parker hired a nanny to assist with the children and

Parker's mother came to live with them to help in any way she could.

In May 2002, the army sent Parker back to Germany to the Barton Barracks, U.S. Army Garrison Ansbach, Installation Management Command, situated in northern Bavaria in the foothills of the Alps. He was assigned as a lieutenant colonel, overseeing a battalion. Parker was thrilled by his return. At a company command ceremony on McGraw Kaserne, a former army installation in Munich, he said, "I am the luckiest man in the world. I feel sorry for anyone who is not me today."

Julie continued on with the medications prescribed during her recent institutionalization. She also made regular visits to her psychiatrist, who added an unspecified personality disorder to her list of mental health diagnoses.

Julie was well enough in 2003 to fly back from Germany with Parker for a special occasion in her hometown of Muscatine. Forty-five years earlier, Patty Peterson and Jim Powers had been wed in Chariton, Iowa, on August 16. Their family gathered round the couple to celebrate their long years of marriage. Julie and Parker were not the only ones who'd traveled a great distance. Julie's brother, David, and his wife, Julie, traveled from Michigan to attend, and Julie's sister, Carol, and her husband, Joe, made the trip from Syracuse, New York, to reunite on that special day. They all enjoyed the celebration of the faithful couple who were the heart and soul of their extended family.

Parker was transferred in April 2005 to U.S. Army Garrison Baden-Würtemberg in Heidelberg in southwest Germany in a steep valley on the river Neckar. It was a picturesque city complete with the perfect romantic symbol, a castle lying in ruins.

Within six months of their arrival on that base, Julie refused to take her medications—a fairly typical reaction by those suffering with bipolar disorder. The drugs needed to minimize the lows of depression at the cost of the highs of the mania often turn the world into a very flat place where nothing can seem to generate any strong emotional response.

Many patients have rebelled against this overly placid state of mind.

Julie had continued to balk against taking her medication when the family returned to the United States, where they purchased a home on Railbed Drive in Odenton, Maryland, and got busy making home improvements.

Julie's nonstop six-month period of mania, caused by her noncompliance with her prescriptions, finally overwhelmed Parker. Along with an unnatural elevation of mood and energy levels, this phase was marked by agitation, irritability, poor temper control, reckless behavior, false beliefs, and poor judgment—a difficult combination of manifestations for any family with a bipolar member to handle on their own. He took Julie to Walter Reed Hospital for treatment of her mental disorders in early 2006.

CHAPTER 10

On August 1, 2006, Parker Schenecker finally received the promotion that had eluded him for so long. He was now Colonel Schenecker. That elevation meant that the Schenecker family was uprooted again. Parker was sent to the U.S. Army War College at Carlisle Barracks, the second-oldest active military base, nestled in the stunning, lush beauty of Pennsylvania's Susquehanna Valley.

The town of Carlisle traced back to prerevolutionary days when it served as the jumping-off point for pioneers and adventurers traveling over the Allegheny Mountains to points west. The first military encampment dated back to 1756, when the site played a prominent role in the French and Indian War.

The onset of the American Revolutionary War spurred the establishment of a more permanent presence with the construction of substantial brick buildings on the grounds. Intense military activity erupted there again in 1794 with the commencement of the Whiskey Rebellion, an uprising by farmers who refused to pay tax on the whiskey they distilled from their corn crops.

When President George Washington traveled there during that conflict, he reviewed a contingent of ten thousand troops. He was impressed by what he saw at Carlisle Barracks and wanted to make it the site of a federal military academy. That honor went, instead, to the state of New York at its West Point location. In addition, during this period of history Carlisle was one of forty sites competing to be the location of the new federal capital.

During the Civil War, the base became a central supply center for the Union forces, providing weapons, ammunition, horses, and quartermaster supplies to the soldiers. In 1863, Confederate forces shelled the town and torched the barracks.

The control of the facility was passed to the Department of Interior in 1879 when the Bureau of Indian Affairs was charged with opening the Carlisle Indian Industrial School, the first boarding school for the education and enculturation of Native American children. Students from the western Indian tribes flocked to the institution for its curriculum that combined an academic program emphasizing English language skills with vocational training to prepare them for successful transition to becoming productive workers in American society.

World War One brought the facility back under the purview of the War Department, and after this conflict it began its reconfiguration as a predominately educational facility with the opening of the Medical Field Service School. At the end of those hostilities, five additional instructional centers opened: the Army Information School, School for Government of Occupied Areas, Chaplain School, Military Police School, and Army Security Agency School.

Finally, in the spring of 1951, the U.S. Army War College moved from Washington, D.C., to Carlisle Barracks. By the time of Parker's arrival, the institution had long established its position as the army's ultimate professional development base, preparing officers for the responsibilities of strategic leadership in a joint, interagency, intergovernment, and international environment.

Parker immersed himself in this inquiry-driven model of graduate study to master the strategic arts in the three different areas: as a leader, a theorist, and a practitioner. He learned about the history of warfare and conflict, in order to understand the underlying causes as well as gain insights for the future, and the universe of existing theory to enhance his ability to develop new strategic concepts for any situation.

Parker and Julie settled their children into a home on Hope Drive in a suburban area about a mile away from the center of the picturesque village of Boiling Springs, wrapped around the serene Children's Lake. Situated on the Appalachian Trail, it was one of the nine towns in the country designated as an Appalachian Trail Community.

The name of the village arose from the natural artesian-well springs in and around the town, the most prominent one known as "the bubble." These formations caused the temperature in the lake to remain at a constant fifty-two degrees Fahrenheit all year round, causing it to steam continuously during the colder-weather months. With fewer than three thousand residents, Boiling Springs projected a warm small-town ambience, with 98 percent of the population white and the remaining portion fragmented into small allotments of black, Native American, Asian, Pacific Islander, and other ethnic groups.

The Schenecker's new neighborhood was a blissful segment of upper-middle-class suburbia built a couple of years earlier on a piece of farmland. It was surrounded on two sides by operating farms. The residents were a blend of young families with small children, middle-aged families with teenagers, and empty nesters and/or retired folks. The houses there were two- to three-thousand square-foot homes in two styles: modern and colonial. The one that Parker and Julie bought was a pretty yellow two-story colonial complete with shutters.

Quiet, small, with little traffic, it was often called Mr. Rogers' Neighborhood by locals. The residents, for the most part, were nice, friendly people who smiled as easily as Mr. Rogers did. Although there were some shopping and dining opportunities a mile away in the village, folks who lived in the Scheneckers' community usually traveled to the larger Carlisle to buy groceries, clothing, and other essentials or to go to a restaurant. Many elected to live in the Boiling Springs area because of its good school district, with small, manageable schools, where their children could feel at home.

Beau Schenecker's personality blossomed in this environment, revealing a likeable and loveable person who quickly made and retained friends worldwide. Although shorter than average for boys his age, he gained stature through his amazing intuition, empathy for others, and a great sense of humor.

One of his friends in his typing class, Emily Corica, sat directly behind him. They goofed around together and during the winter shared the mutual problem of constantly chapped lips. They'd tease each other over their minor affliction, but Emily said she always won those playful battles because Beau's lips were always in worse shape than hers.

A highlight of the time Calyx spent here was her art classes. She learned to work in charcoal, ink and wash, pastels, watercolors, and acrylics. A piece of her work, an illustration of her military family, was entered into the 2007 Armed Services YMCA art contest. Of the twelve grand prize winners across the country, Calyx was the top winner out of all the army entries. She was awarded a five-hundred-dollar U.S. Savings Bond.

From their arrival in this idyllic setting Julie appeared to be doing quite well. She seemed stable and mentally healthy. Parker graduated from the U.S. Army War School in May 2007. They sold their home for $345,000 and the family moved south. Parker's next position was as the deputy NSA (National Security Agency) representative to CENTCOM (Central Command) in Tampa, Florida, at MacDill Air Force Base. He was mainly responsible for the National Security Agency's support to military operations.

In addition to added prestige and responsibility, Parker was now earning in excess of one hundred thousand dollars per year. Despite the Scheneckers' improved economic situation and their envious deployment to a base with balmy winter temperatures and close proximity to the beach, it was here that Julie's mental health faltered and eventually disintegrated.

CHAPTER 11

Tampa, Florida, recently ranked as the fifth-best outdoor city by *Forbes* and as a top city for twentysomethings by the *Washington Square News,* has a diverse history. An influx of Cubans and Spanish workers were brought in to build the cigar industry in 1886. Peak production of 500 million hand-rolled cigars was achieved there in 1929, making Tampa the "Cigar Capital of the World."

That Spanish-speaking population was followed by the arrival of Italian and Eastern European Jewish emigrants who built businesses and shops to serve the cigar workers. When Henry Platt's railroad development led him to erect the Tampa Bay Hotel, a quarter-of-a-mile-long Moorish Revival–style luxury resort, tourism took root and exploded, expanding the influence of that industry in the area.

The hotel and its manicured gardens on the banks of the Hillsborough River stand today but now house the University of Tampa.

When the Scheneckers first arrived in this subtropical city on the picturesque Gulf Coast, they rented a place on Whisper Pointe Drive while they looked to purchase a more permanent home. On May 1, 2008, they bought a house located in North Tampa in the Ashleigh Reserve gated suburban community, at 16305 Royal Park Court. An eight-year-old two-story single-family residence with a

10,584-square-foot lot was priced at $448,000. The Scheneckers made a down payment of approximately $90,000 and obtained a mortgage for the balance. Unfortunately, property values in the state and most particularly in Tampa were about to plummet.

Early in 2008, Julie grew entranced by the writings of German New Age author Eckhart Tolle and his book *A New Earth: Awakening to Your Life's Purpose,* an Oprah Winfrey Book Club selection. His thoughts on page 22 particularly captured Julie's attention:

> *You then no longer derive your identity, your sense of who you are, from the incessant stream of thinking that in the old consciousness you take to be yourself. What a liberation to realize that the "voice in my head" is not who I am. Who am I then? The one who sees that. The awareness that is prior to the thought, the space in which the thought—or the emotion or space perception—happens.*
>
> *Ego is no more than this: identification with form, which primarily means thought forms. If evil has any reality—and it has a relative, not absolute, reality: this is also its definition: complete identification with form—physical forms, thought forms, emotional forms. This results in a total unawareness of my connectedness with the whole, my intrinsic otherness with every "other" as well as with the Source.*
>
> *This forgetfulness is original sin, suffering, delusion.*

Julie logged on to Oprah.com and wrote about this passage: "I used to think I was lulu/split personality because of how much information I could 'download' prior to a thought. This made me sob when I, at 47, was finally validated by the 'space before the thought.' I'm just so grateful to Eckhart for letting me know this is the me that should have been shining all these years."

Julie also relished an earlier work of Tolle's, *The Power of Now.* In it, the author insists that death is an illusion, a mere portal to happiness: "The body that you can see and touch is only a thin, illusory veil. Underneath it, lies the invisible inner body, the doorway into Being, into the Life Unmanifested."

Despite the fact that Tolle sold more than 10 million copies of his book, *Time* magazine referred to the philosophical underpinnings of his work as "spiritual mumbo-jumbo." Christian theologians deemed his work dangerous because he made no distinction between human beings and the deity. Psychiatrists and psychologists were equally alarmed at the possible impact that his teachings would have on those with serious mental health issues, people who are often impacted in a disproportionate manner by religious and spiritual exhortations.

If these writings were a tipping point for Julie, feeding into the psychosis inherent in her schizoaffective disorder, it was not immediately apparent. Certainly her depression came and went during her first year in Tampa, leaving her in a state of lethargy that caused her to ignore housekeeping and meal preparation responsibilities. Only Julie knew whether or not this roller-coaster emotional ride was the result of ineffective pharmaceuticals or caused by her noncompliance with the prescribed instructions of her physician.

Even though the topic of possible divorce came up now and again, Parker and Julie were able to mend fences and move forward. She still demonstrated the signs of a good mother who cheered at the kids' athletic events and learned the latest pop songs to sing along with them when she picked Calyx and Beau up after school.

In 2009, life seemed to hold great promise for the Schenecker family. They'd settled into their new home, the children made friends at school, and Julie gathered a clutch of women friends in the area.

One of Julie's friends, Lorraine Livingston, became a prominent part of her life that year. The two women bowled, played tennis and lunched together, and made each birthday of anyone in their group of friends a special occasion. The group also exchanged gifts over the holidays. One year, Julie presented each one of her friends with stationery with her initials on it. Another time, she gave them all gold necklaces. Lorraine described Julie as a good friend, a lovely woman with unsurpassed elegance.

Lorraine and Julie were also quite active as volunteers, working together for many charitable causes, including the Muscular Dystrophy Association. They volunteered to help out with the Tampa Bay Pro-Am at the Tournament Players Club Tampa Bay in Lutz, Florida, with its Bobby Weed—designed course, in April. The event paired Champion Tour professionals with special guests, celebrities, and local amateur stars to raise money for nonprofit organizations. Over the twenty-four years of the Tampa Bay Pro-Am Foundation's existence, they'd contributed a total of $9 million to many different groups.

The 2009 event raised money for four charities: Diabetic Charitable Services, which aided in early detection of the disease and provided help in monitoring and controlling it; the Child Abuse Council, with its child abuse prevention and family education programs; Everyday Blessings, a child placing and caring agency; and the Judeo Christian Health Clinic, which provided free, compassionate care to indigent Tampa Bay residents. That year was a star-studded tournament. In addition to prominent professional names in the world of golf, such as Hale Irwin, Tom Watson, and Nick Price, a lot of celebrities participated in the event. Comedian Bill Murray played and hit an accidental hook shot that beaned a woman in the head at the ninth hole. Actor Michael J. Fox, a longtime survivor of Parkinson's disease, stirred hearts with his emotional finish on the eighteenth hole. Also golfing in the event were NFL Hall of Famers Emmitt Smith and Jerry Rice and other former NFL players such as Ronde Barber and Vinny Testaverde; comedian George Lopez; singer Vince Gill; actors Kevin Costner and Mark "Marky Mark" Wahlberg; and NBC's Stone Phillips.

Julie and Lorraine got close up to them all when they

worked the Outback Steakhouse Pro-Am Aussie Bash, a private party for sponsors, players, and VIPs on April 13. The party featured heavy hors d'oeuvres, an open bar, and live entertainment by country singer Tim McGraw.

In January 22, 2009, Parker, Julie, and Calyx traveled with Parker's mother, Nancy, to celebrate at a debutante ball. No one noticed any discord between mother and daughter—Julie and Calyx seem to get along wonderfully.

In September of that year, Parker returned to his old high school in Texas, Fort Worth Country Day School, to receive the Service for Humanity Award. They cited his exemplary military service and enumerated the many honors he'd received in his illustrious career: Defense Meritorious Service Medal, Army Meritorious Service Medal, Army Commendation Medal, Air Force Achievement Medal, Southwest Asia Service Medal with a Bronze Service Star, Iraq Campaign Medal, Afghanistan Campaign Medal, Global War on Terrorism Expeditionary Medal, Global War on Terrorism Service Medal, Joint Meritorious Unit Award, Army Superior Unit Medal, National Defense Service Medal, Overseas Ribbon, Army Service Ribbon, the Knowlton Award for Excellence in Army Intelligences, and the German Army Service Cross in Silver.

In October 2009, when Julie returned to Iowa for a reunion with her college basketball team, something about her didn't seem quite right to her old friends. She was far more subdued. "She was not the same bubbly person I had known and I thought her eyes looked a little bit either distant or vacant," teammate Lisa Pilch said, adding that when she'd seen Julie five years earlier at another reunion she'd been her old self.

Still Julie gave no indication that anything was amiss during their time at the restaurant or the UNI football game. She updated everyone about her children's lives and took an active part in conversations, but on reflection, teammate Lisa Pilch thought that Julie never discussed anything in depth.

Nonetheless, when Beau called while the women were at lunch Julie spoke to him like any other mother would talk to her son. She didn't indicate that there were any problems. She gave every appearance of loving her life.

Thanksgiving that year was a family-oriented delight. Parker's mother, Nancy Schenecker, and Julie's parents, Jim and Patty, traveled to Tampa to gather around the family table. Julie's friends dropped by the house that weekend to meet the parents. No conflicts erupted and all seemed well in their world.

Looking back, it was easy to see that this peaceful time was nothing more than the proverbial quiet before the storm. The winds of disaster were gaining strength, pushing the axis of the Schenecker family's world into a critical tilt. It would not be long before everything spun out of control.

CHAPTER 12

After Christmas 2009, Parker posted several photos of his family of four on his Facebook page. One shot was a dramatic black-and-white that caused one of his friends to write: "Did you find the fountain of youth and you're not telling anyone?!!!!"

Another photo, showing all four members of the family donning Santa hats, generated another comment: "Your family is something to be proud of, look at how happy every one of you are!"

Beau had, in his easygoing fashion, made new friends from the moment he arrived in Tampa. He was passionate about playing soccer and was considered an "amazing goalkeeper." He also played on Fusion, a football club team. He could often be seen playing basketball, street hockey, and other sports in the cul-de-sac with Scott Patchan, Calvin Works, and other neighborhood friends.

Like most boys his age, he also liked playing games on the Internet. One of his favorites was Call of Duty, a multiple-player modern warfare game. His list of gaming friends was long and international. One of them, an Ontario teenager, Abraham Nerajan, said, "I only knew him when we played online. But I know for a fact that he was an enthusiastic and generous kid."

Beau attended nearby Liberty Middle School with its bright red tile entrance. Standing right next to it was the nearly identical Freedom High School—the two exteriors being so similar that at first glance they appeared to be one rambling school. Beau planned to shift next door to the other building when he went into ninth grade.

He was playful with his teachers at the middle school, teasing Ms. Daisy Questella about her chewing-gum rule, but he always did his homework and never got a bad grade. Beau was a good student but not as driven as his older sister. All in all, Beau settled into his life in Tampa with a broad network of friends at home and at school. He was spirited, full of fun—an all-American boy.

When Calyx first moved to Tampa, she was not as quick to get into her groove as Beau had been. She felt disconnected from her peers and not quite comfortable with social interactions with others her age. That changed when she entered into the esteemed International Baccalaureate Program at the C. Leon King High School.

The IB Program was an academically challenging and balanced education system designed to prepare students for success at university and life beyond. In addition to honors-level class instruction, the curriculum included three requirements to broaden the educational experience and challenge students in the application of their knowledge: the extended essay, requiring students to perform independent research; Theory of Knowledge, a course encouraging students to understand the different methods of knowing (perception, emotion, language, and reason) and different kinds of knowledge (scientific, artistic, mathematical, and historical); and creativity, action, and service, challenging students to perform real-world tasks outside of the classroom.

Not only did she have a more demanding academic program, but she also had a lot farther to travel to get to class than her brother. The school building was older than his and constructed around an open quadrant of green space. In the front of the building, sidewalks were shaded by towering trees dripping with Spanish moss. Up against the school, crepe myrtle and palm trees softened the institutional feel of the place.

In her freshman year, Calyx crossed paths with Jena Young, Sara Wortman, and Tatiana Henry. The three girls had all attended different middle schools and felt as estranged from teen society during those years as Calyx had. Jena didn't feel as if she fit in, Sara had no girlfriends, and Tatiana hid her love for the Harry Potter books, concerned about what others might think of her.

They'd spent all their lives in Tampa and were entranced by Calyx, the girl from all over the world—a military daughter who had attended more schools than she could remember. They loved her exotic fashion sense demonstrated in a number of her outfits, including a dress with a zipper that went all the way down her arm and a jacket from Korea.

Calyx was tall and thin, with scattered freckles across her face, and wore her long hair twisted in an effortless bun. And she wasn't at all quiet about her obsession with Harry Potter. The subject arose in study hall with Tatiana, much to the other girl's delight at their shared fascination. She talked about the books in Spanish class with Sara and in homeroom with Jena. Calyx suggested they all start hanging together.

In no time, the four were inseparable. She had roots nowhere, yet, oddly, it was she who solidified their relationship. The four called themselves the Ostuaries after Calyx nearly convinced the others that "ostuary" was a word used to designate a genetic cross between an ostrich and a cassowary.

At the core of their relationships with each other was their shared, consuming fascination with and passion for the Harry Potter books by J. K. Rowling.

Just what was the real draw of this series—the underlying reasons that this series spawned such undying devotion? Rowling said that the major theme of the series is death: "My books are largely about death. They open with the death of

Harry's parents. There is Voldemart's obsession with conquering death and his quest for immortality at any price."

Many academics have pointed to the corollary with the journey through adolescence and harrowing ordeals to acceptance. Whatever spell Rowling wove as she wrote, it was no wonder that Calyx, Jena, Tatiana, and Sara were besotted with the Harry Potter books—they had magic, tragedy, and a compelling battle between good and evil.

Calyx led the group in their efforts to start a Harry Potter fan club. Jeff Halle, the English teacher who sponsored the Harry Potter fan club, said, "She was exceptionally sweet. She was respectful. She was the kind of girl that if I had a daughter and I could pick which one, I would choose her."

By the end of the year, Calyx and her friends recruited a group of fourteen kids to meet on a soccer field and recreate an earthbound game of Quidditch, a competition that, in the books, required flying brooms. The girls came as close as they could in real life, using duct tape and Hula-hoops to build goalposts and balls closer to earth and substituting water balloons for the bludger, a ball that, in the books, was used to knock players off their broomsticks. Calyx, the fastest of the four girls, was the human substitute for the golden snitch, an elusive ball with wings that brought victory to the team that captured it. With a one-minute head start, no one could catch Calyx.

During school spirit week in October 2010, all four girls dressed up like students at Hogwarts School from the Harry Potter books. One of Calyx's dreams was to plant a willow on the King High School campus as a tribute to the Whomping Willow that disguised a secret passageway from J. K. Rowling's Hogwarts School to the Shrieking Shack. Another wish destined never to be fulfilled was the desire for more Harry Potter. Fans had another book-based movie in their future, but J. K. Rowling said she would not write another book in the series. For fans like Calyx, Tatiana, Jena, and Sarah hope that the author would change her mind ran through their dreams.

CHAPTER 13

Although the four Ostuaries had Harry Potter and a lot of
other things in common, each girl was still a distinctive individual. Jena was artsy, loved sci-fi, striped hoodies, and
plaid pants. Sara, the always punctual one, liked math, physics, and architecture. She spent endless hours Googling
about anything and everything that captured her imagina-
tion. The "mom" of the group was the nurturing Tatiana.
She always carried a big purse, allowing the other girls to
stow wallets and other belongings in it, when they ran
around together.

Calyx's constant companions were all aware of Beau and
knew that Calyx was very protective of him. Once when she
was out with her friends and Beau was at home alone, she
thought she'd forgotten to lock the door when she left. Immediately she dropped what she was doing and called to make
sure he was okay and get him to lock the door.

Beau would play games on the computer in the office
area on the second floor. If Calyx had her chat open and one
of her friends popped on and said: "Hello, Beau," the young
teenager would be embarrassed by the older girl's attention
and walk away from the computer.

On the other hand, the girls barely knew Julie. Calyx
didn't like to talk about her mother, and the girls didn't push
her to do so. When girls needed rides, it was Calyx's father,

Colonel Parker Schenecker, who usually showed up. The four sat on docks, explored parks, watched *The Office,* and video-chatted together.

When Calyx's class had a field trip downtown, she asked if the rest of the inseparable four could come, too. The teacher agreed and the girls brought along a camera, setting the timer so they could get pictures of the four of them together. They viewed the architecture of Sacred Heart Church and the Curtis Hixson Waterfront Park in Tampa. They ice-skated under any conditions the winter brought, and when it rained they didn't care.

At the end of the day, Latanya Henry and Parker showed up to pick up the four girls. The adults fussed over the kids, lamenting their resistance to using umbrellas. While they talked, Parker wrapped his arm around Calyx to keep her warm.

Parker, not Julie, was the parent who showed up to unload tables for an early-morning fund-raising yard sale. He was the one who drove the girls home from Jena's place on the beach. Before high school homecoming, Parker dropped Calyx off at The Cheesecake Factory and then took Beau to dinner at the California Pizza Kitchen.

Some of Julie's lack of involvement came from the fact that Calyx did not want to ask her mother for rides since she often got in trouble when she pushed last-minute plans on Julie. When her dad was out of town, Calyx got grounded a lot. But the teenager did try to get along and minimize friction with her mother. According to biology teacher David d'Albany, if Calyx was talking with someone—even a teacher—at pickup time and her mother rang her cell phone, "Calyx would drop everything and rush to her mom."

Calyx's friends had no idea that a deteriorating relationship and rising conflict with her mother were behind her reasons for applying to boarding school. They thought it was prompted by the C that Calyx received in a class during her freshman year. They were unaware that anything was seriously wrong in the Schenecker home. Their parents, however, were a bit more cued into the reality of the situation.

Sara's dad urged her to invite Calyx over a couple of days during each school week just to get her out of the stressful house and give her a break from her mom.

Calyx excelled at track and cross-country. It was not easy to balance the challenging academic demands of the International Baccalaureate Program with the physical exertion and time commitments required by pursuing this sport, but Calyx managed it well.

Her coach Gary Bingham said that, at the time, she was "the fastest freshman I ever had." He said that Calyx was quirky and fascinated by bugs and funny-looking leaves on running trails. She'd stop to pick up acorns, insects, and other items that caught her attention during practice. "She was easygoing and bubbly—smart, too," he said.

While she was a freshman, the coach got to know her mother, Julie. He thought she was an attentive and supportive mother—one who picked her daughter up from practice, cheered through track meets, and attended team suppers. On one occasion, Julie even brought Coach Bingham a birthday present. It wasn't until Calyx's sophomore year that Julie faded out of the picture.

Calyx was a determined and tenacious athlete, too. Even when hurting legs brought her to tears during the homestretch of a race, she pushed herself forward to cross the finish line because she knew her team needed her. In the spring season of her freshman year, she was gratified by achieving three personal bests.

In competition in the University of South Florida/George M. Steinbrenner International, on March 30, she ran in the 400-meter dash. She came in thirty-ninth place, but with her time of under one minute and eight seconds it was the quickest that she ever recorded. One week later, at the Western Conference National Division, she placed twelfth in the 800-meter race—crossing the finish line in under two minutes and forty-seven seconds, racking up another high point of her track career. She topped it all off on April 1 with her performance in the 1600-meter run at the Florida High

School Athletic Association's event. With a time of less than six minutes and two seconds, she came in at eighth place. And she still had three more years in high school to improve her personal times and raise her rank in the sport.

October 2010 marked another achievement in Calyx's athletic career. She was pumped by her team's chances of having an unsurpassed season. In the Little Everglades Pre-State Invitational, she achieved her best time ever in the 5000-meter run, finishing in less than twenty-one and a half minutes.

It wasn't just in track and cross-country where she propelled herself to greater challenges. Calyx also liked to climb rock walls without wearing a harness. She was involved in charitable causes, participating in the King High School Relay For Life in March of 2010. Her father went with her and walked the track at her side all night long. At one point, Parker lost sight of Calyx but then found her, sound asleep in the bounce house, oblivious to the blaring music and the endless sound of footsteps lapping around the track.

Calyx had the added dimension of being a published artist, who dazzled teachers with her artwork, excelling at both painting and sculpting. She often requested creative assignments from her art teachers so that she could show them what she could do. She signed all of her work with a big *C* punctuated by a small *x*.

She relished her academic accomplishments, too, throwing herself into the highest-level classes at her school. An intense desire to learn and her wonderment at all life had to offer was energizing and uplifting. She was also an active participant in the speech and debate clubs.

Principal Carla Bruning described Calyx as an excellent student who was "popular, sweet and enthusiastic. . . . She was a great kid, the kind you would want to clone."

Calyx, like many teenagers, was a bit short on self-confidence. She became embarrassed when complimented. Praise about a drawing could make her ball up a sketch. Nice words about her interesting choice of clothing could cause her to cover up a funky outfit. If a boy asked her to dance, her face automatically contorted into a big-eyed, freaked-out expression.

She quickly backed away if she thought she was putting someone out, saying, "I'm-sorry-I'm-sorry-I'm-sorry." If she feared that she was upsetting someone, she'd try to take back her words, saying, "Just-kidding-just-kidding-just-kidding."

But with her troop of friends she entered a comfort zone. She felt free enough to proudly paint a lightning-bolt scar on her forehead and got the other girls to do the same.

There was something about the intensity of the relationship among Calyx, Tatiana, Sara, and Jena—a level of commitment to one another that appeared to go beyond typical high school alliances. Three of the girls pointed to Calyx as their guiding light and the superglue that held their friendship fast. They were certain that nothing could ever tear them apart.

On September 12, 2010, Calyx celebrated one of life's milestones—her sixteenth birthday year. Sara Wortman and her mother baked red velvet cupcakes, one of the birthday girl's favorites, to celebrate the occasion.

Another upcoming event on Calyx's school year calendar was slated for May. A member of the Reading Rocks Million Words Club at the high school, she was one of the planners for the club picnic.

She was also involved in using her track talents for a loftier goal. She planned for next spring's Run For Life to benefit the American Cancer Society. She began forming her team, which she called the Wizarding Independence Day team. She even presented a research paper to Kathryn Smith, the faculty manager of the event, justifying the name by arguing that it was an actual holiday. Calyx made a commitment to be the number one fundraiser out of the fifty groups participating in the event. She and her teammates set a goal of raising $7,777.77—since seven was the most powerfully magical number in J. K. Rowling's Harry Potter books.

* * *

Despite—or maybe because of—the conflict in her home life, Calyx had big dreams for her future. She wanted to attend three different colleges at one time to cherry-pick the best opportunities from her higher education. She wanted to live in New York City when she was grown. She also longed to see the elephants in Thailand, and she wanted to learn how to train them. She planned to run a marathon in that country to benefit orphans. She thought she could live in the Big Apple for most of the year and spend her summers among the elephants.

As Calyx grew, matured, and developed a better understanding of herself and the world, Julie seemed to be losing any understanding and perspective of her purpose in life and her relationship to those around her. As Calyx strained toward the seemingly limitless possibilities in her future, Julie grew more and more disconnected from her children and from family life in general.

CHAPTER 14

Julie's deepening emotional remoteness from her family went unnoticed by those outside of the family home during their first two years in Tampa. They did not suspect that beneath that smiling, happy veneer an ugly undercurrent flowed toward disaster.

On May 7, 2010, one of Julie's more than four hundred Facebook friends wrote Mother's Day wishes to all mothers, complimenting them for their bravery. "Not sure how you do it, but glad you do."

Julie commented on that sentiment, writing: "Some days, not sure how we do it, either!! ☺"

On August 24, Julie Liked a friend's link, reading: "Be kinder than necessary, because everyone you meet is fighting some sort of battle." There was no indication that any of her Facebook friends had any inkling of the intensity of Julie's losing battle with her mental health and substance abuse.

A friend caught Julie's interest on September 23 when she posted a quotation from Henry Ward Beecher: "Hold yourself to a higher standard than anybody else expects of you."

Julie wrote an appreciative comment: "I needed that advice today—have a 16 yr old daughter!"

Still Julie had some maternal connection to her daughter. Julie posted a number of images of Calyx running on the track and group photos with her cross-country team. In one photograph posted by Julie's husband, daughter Calyx Schenecker is seen posing with six other team members. Julie posted a comment on Parker's page: "That's my baby! doin' something I could never do—3.2 miles!!"

Julie responded to a friend whose status said: 'It's Mommy Week! Post the day you became a Mommy," writing: "calyx powers 9/12/94 in Germany and powers beau 9/29/97 in Honolulu!"

She marked "Like" on posts about motherhood from two different friends. One read: "If God blessed you with a child and you are forever thankful, press like." Another said: "If you hurt my daughter, I will make your death look like an accident."

That year, Julie reminisced on Facebook about skiing in Austria in the late eighties. She posted a new favorite phrase: "Dear Lord, please keep your arm around my shoulder and your hand over my mouth . . . Amen."

As 2010 progressed, Julie fell deeper and deeper under the control of her psychological demons, landing in a severe depression that caused her to withdraw from friends and family. Her descent was accentuated by a series of surgeries. When they were completed, she was addicted to painkillers, in particular OxyContin. Her drug abuse made a difficult situation even worse. Parker was aware of this substance abuse and also knew she was drinking heavily at home during the day. Parker forbad Julie from driving the car with her children because of her frequent intoxication and her obvious mental instability.

In early October 2010, on the way home from cross-country practice, Calyx was driving and Julie was in the front passenger seat. They stopped at the supermarket. Julie waited in the car. When Calyx returned with her sack, Julie peered inside it.

Calyx snapped, "Don't look in my grocery sack!"

Julie backhanded her daughter in the face and continued to slap her with an open hand over a thirty-second period.

When Calyx reached the gate of their community, Julie slapped her again. Calyx grabbed her mother's hand to stop her. Calyx's face was red, but her sunglasses shielded her from any serious injury.

At first Calyx kept the information to herself. However, while attending counseling for three weeks at the Children's Crisis Center in Tampa she finally blurted out the incident on November 2. Her counselor reported it to law enforcement.

Four days later, police responded to the home to investigate the allegation of child abuse. They saw no visible injuries on Calyx, but the girl told them that her mother hit her so hard in the mouth a month earlier that it caused bleeding.

Julie claimed that Calyx told her: "Stay out of my business," "You're disgusting," and, "You're not my parent." Julie said she "backhanded her daughter three times for being disrespectful." And that her daughter "was not bruised or bleeding" during the incident.

Officer Julie Becker wrote: "Calyx said she was never hit like this before. She is usually disciplined by getting her privileges or belongings taken away from her." She added that during the interview Calyx "seemed cautious of what she was saying and at times began to cry." Calyx, she said, "was hoping for a solution between her and her mom" by reporting the incident.

Tampa Police Department spokesperson Laura McElroy said, "Parents can discipline their children using physical force, as long as there's no injury. That's why there was no criminal offense at that time."

Because of this legal loophole, no criminal charges were filed against Julie although she admitted to hitting her daughter. Often in life, as in novels, the foreshadowing is missed until it's too late.

CHAPTER 15

According to the Florida Highway Patrol, on November 8, 2010, at 11:00 a.m., Julie Schenecker caused a two-vehicle collision. She had pushed her car up to 70 miles per hour in a 55 mph zone. As her Mercedes approached a landscaping truck that was pulling a trailer filled with lawn mowers and other yard equipment, she couldn't or wouldn't stop. Either she did not see the vehicle ahead or she could not react in time. Her Mercedes slammed into the rear of the vehicle. The trailer came unhitched, rolling away in one direction with the pickup that was hauling it ending up on a median strip facing oncoming traffic.

The officer on the scene wrote that Julie "showed signs of drug impairment" and had "dilated pupils with no reaction to light" and "mush-mouthed speech." She was transported to the hospital. When police finished at the scene and went to the hospital to get blood alcohol levels as well as a sample for drug testing, she had already left and they were unable to do a sobriety test. At the time, it was believed that Julie was intoxicated from drinking and also under the influence of OxyContin.

The crash caused bodily injury to the people in the other vehicle and $26,500 in property damage. She was cited for careless driving and ordered to pay a $151 fine and to attend traffic school. Had the officers been able to ascertain her substance abuse, she would have fared much worse. Once again, she slid past the worst consequences for her actions.

Parker was furious. He had told her many times not to drive while she was under the influence. She'd made many promises to quit her drug and alcohol abuse. This incident fired up all his fears and concerns that she'd cause an accident that would harm or kill one or both of the children.

In frustration he kicked her out of their home, and she spent the next two nights on her own in a local hotel. Two days later, Parker picked her up from the hotel and drove her straight to a substance abuse rehabilitation center in Clearwater where she spent twenty-one days being treated for prescription drug abuse. While she was gone, Parker's mother, Nancy, stayed in the home with the children. Parker got other family members to help him take care of the children when extra assistance was needed.

In the midst of all this family chaos, Sara Wortman sent a handwritten note to Parker and Julie Schenecker on November 12. Its silly, lighthearted tone indicated that Calyx had not informed her friends that her mother was not in the home or anything had gone wrong in the last week.

"The time has come for the first part of the epic finale of a generation," Sara began. She described Calyx as an "excellent student" and expressed her empathy for the stress that high achievement created. Then, she expressed her feeling that her friend deserved "a day off" on Friday, November 19, to view the movie, *Harry Potter and the Deathly Hollows Part I,* with Sara and the other Ostuaries.

"Think about it," she wrote. "Would you really want Calyx at school if she could not pay full attention in class? Also, if you allow her to skip school, she will be far happier and in a much better mood." She reminded the Scheneckers that with family coming for Thanksgiving, it would be preferable to have a "happy Calyx" in her home. She then argued that since Calyx was a teenager, it was her right to have fun occasionally. If they denied this privilege to Calyx, she warned it could hurt their relationship with their daughter.

She signed the note as Calyx's "friend, classmate and colleague."

While Julie was away in the rehab facility, Parker contacted her physician to get information so that he would know what he should do when she returned home to reunite with the family. But the doctor said, "Because of HIPAA [Health Insurance Portability and Accountability Act] laws, I can't discuss it with you."

Parker didn't know how he could be expected to make the right decisions without knowing more about the nature of his wife's current mental state. On December 3, just before Julie was about to check out of the rehab facility, Parker sent her an e-mail, hoping to convince her that disclosure from her mental health professionals would be in the best interests of the whole family. "Pls consider executing a release for [the doctor] to speak with me."

Julie's response did not give him much hope for her upcoming return to home: "hell no! sorry about your luck."

Parker tried to persuade her once again. He sent her a measured and reasonable response: "I think if you asked him, he'd say that he would like to and that it would be helpful. He would help with some ideas on how to improve things while keeping your private issues private. . . . I believe it's critical for us (all four of us) to get into family counseling immediately. Since you feel ganged up on, this situation will quickly spin out of control without it." A more prescient line had never been written.

CHAPTER 16

When Julie returned home, the same patterns emerged. She was still abusing alcohol and OxyContin despite her stint in rehab. She cut off any contact with friends or family members. She didn't even attempt to interact with her husband or children. Typically, she spent twenty hours a day in bed, lost in a severe, dark depression. Ironically, despite the amount of sleep she had, Julie still remained tired and drained of energy—a situation quite common in a bipolar individual in the midst of a depressive phase.

On December 6, Julie e-mailed Parker. She wrote about an upcoming appointment with a mental health counselor and asked whether she should bring the children along. "That's what rehab was all about. . . . Figuring out what my plan for success is . . . Calyx is too pissed at me—worse than before the accident."

Parker responded by admitting that although it was possible that he was wrong when he told her not to return home and immediately ask Calyx and Beau for forgiveness, he still believed that the situation demanded actions, not a prettily worded apology. He then criticized her behavior. He took issue with the amount of time she stayed in her room sleeping and with her determination not to blend back in with the family until his mother ended her stay in the home. That, he wrote, was what was behind his comment that she was sealing her fate with the kids. It recommended family counseling and cautioned that neither she nor the kids could change overnight.

He wrapped up his email with his main concern: "I MUST protect them; they are telling me that they feel unsafe. This is the basic responsibility of a parent, especially a father. . . . . They've asked their father for protection. The hard part of this is that they've asked for protection from their mother."

After Julie spent a week in family therapy at Parker's request, he said that life in their home grew stable, comfortable, and nearly normal. Together, they all gathered in the driveway to wash the cars. A playful sponge fight erupted and soon all four were engaged in a sopping-wet battle, laughing, giggling, and appearing to be a normal, happy family.

During the days before Christmas, "Julie's energy was low, but it was peaceful," Parker said.

In a follow-up to the child abuse investigation instigated in November, caseworkers from the Florida Department of Children & Families visited during this more serene time. When they arrived, the children were wrapping gifts and eagerly anticipating Christmas morning. The household portrayed every indication of normalcy.

Parker and Julie told the caseworkers that the family was in counseling and, on being questioned, said that there was no history of domestic violence. Parker never mentioned any of the past incidents when Julie hit him in front of the children. Both Beau and Calyx told the social workers that they felt safe at home.

Parker said, "My daughter is very angry and at times can be very disrespectful. I often play peacemaker in the home, but I don't mind doing that."

Julie said, "Calyx's behavior had changed since she started attending King High School." Brushing off the slapping incident, Julie added, "I have had to increase my level of discipline since my daughter no longer responds to her privileges being confiscated."

The report filed by the Department of Children & Families, dated December 23, 2010, read: "The overall risk to the children at this time is low. . . . The mother and child have not been in any other altercations and the two have agreed to disagree."

Calyx took on the responsibility of decorating the family tree. On Christmas day, Julie didn't linger in bed; she rose and unwrapped Christmas gifts with the family. Beau got a new laptop from his parents and Calyx received a breathtaking gift: a trip to Thailand the next summer—the first step in making her dream life a tangible concept. Julie and Calyx prepared the holiday dinner together, working like a team, side by side, as they coordinated the preparation of dishes and served them with a flourish.

It all painted a traditional portrait of family harmony, giving every outward appearance that life in the Schenecker household was back on firm ground. All, however, was not what it seemed. Christmas 2010 was the first time ever that Julie had not participated in decorating the home for the holidays. It was the first Christmas that she had not purchased any presents for her family or friends. It was not the same Julie her friends and colleagues had known—not by a long shot.

Parker wanted to believe that Julie was improving during the Christmas holidays. He seemed to believe that Julie could resolve her problems through determination and attitude. To cling to that belief he would have to deny the immutable realties of serious mental illness and the distinct possibility that past behavior could be a predictor for future escalation.

CHAPTER 17

In early January, the Schenecker family attended an Al-Anon meeting for families where about twenty people were in attendance. Calyx rose to her feet, the first person to address the group. She said, "My mom . . . ," but she choked up before saying anything more.

The people gathered around her understood the intensity of her emotions. They sat, patiently and compassionately, waiting for her to compose herself and continue. She tried to start again, "My mom . . . ," and once more she faltered, bursting into tears that broke nearly every heart in the room.

Parker stood. Taking over for his distraught daughter, he said, "We are here because of their mother. She has a drug and alcohol problem and we are here to cope with it."

One of the women attending the meeting exhibited the group's positive response to Parker by saying that he "was just like any normal dad. He was there to help his kids."

On January 11, Parker received orders for a ten-day deployment to the Middle East. Concerned about leaving Julie with the children, he talked to his wife. He wanted to know if everything would be all right while he was gone.

Julie said, "I can handle things for that short period of time."

Parker, who had had trust and honor instilled in him

throughout his collegiate and military career, accepted her words at face value. As a result, he did not ask his commanding officers for a delay that would have surely have been granted due to the family hardship. He knew his wife was depressed, but he reasoned that she had suffered periods of depression previously and this one didn't seem any different from the others.

Julie's brother, Dave, sent her an e-mail on January 14: "Hope you had a nice birthday yesterday! We plan on coming to Florida again during Spring Break. First full week of April."

Dave suspected that his sister was depressed again. He hoped that news of his family's upcoming visit would raise her spirits.

On January 15, Parker sent an e-mail to his and Julie's family and a few close friends. Its content indicated that he had received some criticism for his decisions and how he was handling the situation with Julie.

He began his missive by expressing appreciation for their concern and their willingness to rush to his home in an emergency situation and to visit for the purpose of aiding the family with their day-to-day situation. He quickly switched gears, chastising them for their judgmental attitudes about his parenting decisions and how he was handling the family problems. "I'll write off your criticism as ignorance," he continued, asking them to give some thought to the issues he faced.

"Julie was broken BEFORE I met her. She knew beforehand, but did not tell me." As a result, he said, he'd spent more than twenty years taking on more burden in the relationship than he had expected. He then asked a series of questions. "Have you ever lived with someone with Bipolar Disorder?," "Have you ever lived with a 50-year-old who has the judgment of a 10-year-old?," "Have you ever lived with an alcoholic/addict? I've lived with two of them," "Have you ever had to deal with your spouse hitting you in front of your children? Have you ever had to deal with your spouse hitting

your child in the face while your child was driving the car?"
After each query, he followed up with a second question:
"Did you stay in that relationship or leave?"

For those who answered that they stayed, he wrote that
they had his respect and sympathy and asked for their insight on the problems they had faced. He wrapped up with
an admonishment to his relatives. "I don't need folks taking
shots or lobbing grenades over the wall at me or my children. I don't want your pity, but I DESERVE your respect.
What I don't deserve is your judgment. . . . Just remember,
the most obvious and simple solutions work in math, but
usually not in human relationships."

On January 16, Julie responded to her brother's e-mail about
an upcoming visit: "Sounds great—tho I don't know our
spring break dates yet. I hope we time it right. Did Julie
[Dave's wife] get a little box from me? Didn't even put a note
on it—shame on me!"

The next day, Julie e-mailed her brother: "Please fwd me the
'letter' parker [wrote] to all the family. THX. he went to [Af-
ghanistan] today for 10 days."

Dave wrote back a refusal to send her Parker's email. He
changed the subject, telling her that her emails had gotten
sloppy, incoherent and disturbing. He reminded her that
she was confined without any clothing and belongings because of the fear she would commit suicide and yet every
time she returned home she was welcomed back by her
husband and her children.

He wanted to know why she wasn't grateful for that and
asked why she no longer appreciated all that Parker had
given her and the children. He asked why she didn't talk any
more about the exotic vacations Parker provided for her and
the family. He agreed with her complaint that Parker was
career-oriented, but reminded her that she knew that before
she married him. He also said the whole family knew of
Parker's goal to follow in his grandfather's footsteps and become a general, just as he had done.

He asked her to remember that Parker "has had a 'Generals Party' for the last umpteen years" and expressed his surprise that Parker said he would abandon all of his ambitions. "Here is a guy who is giving up his dream, after 27 dedicated years of serving our country. He's walking away from it all. And to do what? A political agenda? Something bigger? No, to stay in one spot because his family wants him to . . . If Parker doesn't make it to General . . ." no ". . . matter how close he's gotten or what all he's done. His opinion of himself would be, is that 'HE FAILED TO ACCOMPLISH HIS MISSION'."

Dave ended his email by telling his story that although he was willing to travel to Florida to help her and her family, he would not come down to run errands and shuttle the children to activities. He would only come down to play a role in resolving the serious issues if all four family members were willing to participate, but he did not believe that she was willing to make the smallest effort toward making any of the necessary changes or accommodations.

CHAPTER 18

On January 18, after consultation with Calyx's therapist and her high school guidance counselor, the Florida Department of Children & Families determined that the Schenecker children were safe in their home environment. They closed the case file.

Before Parker left Tampa on his temporary deployment to the Middle East, he said his good-byes to his children, telling them both that he loved them to infinity. The kids responded in their traditional, playful way.

Calyx said, "I love you infinity plus one."

Beau followed up, saying, "I love you infinity plus two."

Julie's sister, Carol Walsh, sent an e-mail to Parker, telling him that on January 20 Julie asked her to forward Parker's family e-mail dated January 15. Julie told her that she needed it because she wanted to share it with her counselor. Carol added: "The uncertainty of not knowing what you wrote is probably more distressing to her than what you actually wrote."

Parker wrote back encouraging Carol, agreeing with her assessment. He urged her to forward the message to Julie.

Carol continued the communication writing her assurances to Parker that she knew he was doing his best to deal with all the problems that arose with this family and acknowledged that he was bearing all of the burden. She told him that Julie was feeling all alone and expressed a desire for Parker to talk to her. Carol empathized with Parker about the difficulty to talking to someone who was severely depressed but urged him to do so. Carol wrote, "She conveyed to us months ago that she had lost her relationship with Calyx and if she loses her relationship with you, my biggest concern is her giving up, because she feels she has nothing left, and committing suicide."

She referred to an earlier email where she asked Parker: "Or do you not care anymore and are done?" and explained that she did not mean that as a criticism, but she just wanted to know if he was still committed to the marriage. If twenty years of struggle with Julie's problems was all he could endure, she assured him that she would understand and not place the blame at his feet. On the other hand, she did want him to know that Julie believed that the recent years of their marriage *"had been the best."*

She closed her message by assuring him that as long as he was there and willing to help Julie "move forward," she would not force her way into the situation. Unless he or Julie asked for her to come help, she would stay away. On the other hand, she wrote, "If you can't make things work out or just can't do it anymore, please let me know, as I will step into the picture." She went on to assure him that her consistent message to Julie had been that she was the only one who could affect the necessary changes and the rest of them were powerless without her cooperation. "But I think she does need your help."

Arriving at his destination overseas that day, Parker sent an e-mail to his family to let them know he had arrived safely. Over the next few days, Parker traveled to various locations in Afghanistan.

Julie wrote in her journal about her children: "They are disrespectful and I'm going to take care of it."

On Saturday, January 22, she traveled forty-four miles to

and from her home to Lock N Load Gun Store at 3711 Tampa Road in Oldsmar, Florida. There were a number of weapon stores much closer to her home, but that location had the advantage of being in a different county from her place of residence, making her visit less likely to come to the attention of anyone she knew.

When she reached the front door of the establishment she tugged on the handle, but it was locked for security reasons. A moment later, the buzzer sounded, the door released, and, pulling on it again, Julie gained entry to the store.

Gerald Tanso, the fifty-five-year-old shop owner, and his assistant, sixty-five-year-old Ralph Monaco, were behind the counter when she arrived. Julie said, "I want to purchase a handgun because there have been four or five home invasion robberies in my subdivision recently and I need some protection."

She specifically stated that she wanted to buy a revolver, adding, "My husband is in the military and he's deployed away from the home for thirty days. I was in the military for five years, stationed in Germany, and I loved it there."

Julie pointed to the weapons in the case that caught her eye. Monaco pulled out three different guns and placed them on the counter for her to examine. She handled them all and appeared to be familiar with the operation of each one. She looked "perfectly fine and showed no outward signs of being either emotionally or physically disturbed." She spoke calmly, with no outward signs of nervousness. She spoke clearly and didn't display any speaking problems at all.

She selected a Smith & Wesson blue steel .38-caliber snub-nosed revolver. She filled out the required paperwork, part 1 of the Bureau of Alcohol, Tobacco, Firearms and Explosives Firearms Transaction Form 4473, in a legible but rather sloppy hand. It required answers to a number of questions.

a. "Are you the actual buyer of the gun?" Julie checked "yes."

b. "Are you under indictment in any court for a felony

or other crime for which the judge could imprison you for more than one year?" Julie indicated she was not.

c. "Have you ever been convicted in any court of a felony or any other crime for which the judge could have imprisoned you for more than one year, even if you received a shorter sentence including probation?" She answered: "No."

d. "Are you a fugitive from justice?" Again, she appropriately checked the "no" box.

e. "Are you an unlawful user of, or addicted to, marijuana or any depressant, stimulant, narcotic drug, or any other controlled substance?" Julie checked "no," pointing to a distinct flaw in the system. Did authorities or gun sellers really think that an addict or illegal substance user who wants a firearm would willingly admit to a problem that could block their desired purchase?

f. "Have you ever been adjudicated mentally defective OR have you ever been committed to a mental institution?" Again she misrepresented her history, evading the intent of the question by hanging her answer on the legal fine point that she was not technically, formally "committed," and responded in the negative.

g. "Have you been discharged from the Armed Forces under dishonorable conditions?" Another "no."

h. "Are you subject to a court order restraining you from harassing, stalking or threatening your child or intimate partner?" "No," once again.

Julie continued on answering in the negative to the remaining questions about her citizenship status. She was disappointed to learn that she could not take the revolver with her when she left the store.

"There's a waiting period for the approval of your purchase by the FDLE [Florida Department of Law Enforcement]," Tanso said.

Julie paid for the handgun with her personal credit card

and returned to her home. People who talked to her that day said she was "articulate and perfectly normal." No one knew that, upon reaching home after her trip to the gun store, she pulled out the journal she kept in a blue spiral notebook and wrote: "The massacre will have to be delayed."

CHAPTER 19

At one time, Julie was an early riser eager to face the day. Now that had all changed. She told her fellow car poolers that she didn't like to get up early in the morning and wanted to do the return run from King High School.

Much to the surprise of acquaintances and friends, around January 23 Julie started wearing ripped jeans and revealing blouses—more like a teenager than a fifty-year-old mother. It raised eyebrows, but nothing more.

Dave Powers sent his sister another e-mail the day after she made her first trip to the gun store: "Sorry I haven't called to follow up on this email. . . . I would like you to respond to the various points put forth by me. I would like to see YOUR response to each and every item I discussed. . . . Please respond."

During his absence, Parker communicated with Calyx, Beau, and Julie via e-mail, Skype videoconference, and instant messaging. One of those days, Parker made a phone call to the home to speak to Calyx about an e-mail she'd sent him about her high school course schedule for the following semester. According to Parker, Julie answered the phone and spoke to him without revealing that anything was out of the ordinary at home. Julie, he believed, sounded fine. Since her arrest, however, Julie has denied that that conversation ever occurred.

* * *

On Monday morning, January 24, Beau overslept and missed his ride to school. He woke his mother and asked her to give him a ride to class. Julie told him that she didn't feel like it.

Later that day, Lisa Prisco, Julie's good friend, called to ask how she was doing. Initially, Julie made a noncommittal response about her forgetfulness.

"Julie, you really need to tell your doctor about that. And you need to get therapy," Lisa urged.

"We are all going to counseling. We are really trying, Lisa. But," Julie added, "I do not like the counselor."

"Why not?"

"And I can't remember things," she complained.

"Well, your doctor has prescribed a lot of different medications for your depression and all. Julie, you need to tell your doctor about this. And if you write down what you're saying—that will help you remember."

"And the doctor I saw after my accident, gave me Percocet and hydrocodone."

"Does your regular doctor know you're taking those medications, too?" Lisa asked, but Julie changed the subject.

Parker used Skype to make contact with the home front on January 26. He spoke to and saw Beau, who was sitting on the upstairs sofa using the laptop computer he received for Christmas. Parker also spoke to Calyx. Both of his children seemed to be happy. Neither one of them communicated any concerns or fears about their safety. Parker thought all was well and despite his natural, ever present, parental worries, he had no immediate concerns for their welfare.

CHAPTER 20

Wednesday in English class, Calyx wrote an essay: "In life, the journey proves to be more meaningful than the end, and the way you live exposes your own true personality."

That afternoon, at track practice, Calyx, normally a distance runner, decided that her long legs might be perfect for hurdles and she would give them a try. On her first attempt, she went over a hurdle and fell face-first. She got up laughing and said to Coach Bingham, "Let's go again."

The determined young woman seemed ready to take on any challenge. On this day, at this time, it appeared as if there were no way she could ever be stopped.

Beau had some excitement that day, too. When he saw his teacher Daisy Questella that afternoon, he asked, "Did you know I made the soccer team?"

Daisy smiled at him and said, "Congratulations, Beau."

"Good-bye, I'll see you tomorrow," he said as he left her classroom.

The next day was Thursday, January 27, 2011. Calyx's and Beau's father, Colonel Parker Schenecker, left Afghanistan for redeployment back to the United States, making a scheduled stop in Doha, Qatar. From there he sent e-mails to Julie, Calyx, Beau, his brother, Edmund, his mother-in-law, and a family friend. "Made it back to Q tonight (Thur.) Going to sleep now. Love, Dad/P."

Both children were excited about his imminent return.

Thursday morning, Julie sat down with her friend Lorraine for a short visit before running her errands. Lorraine realized that Julie was depressed that day, but she'd seen her in that state before. Nothing about Julie's behavior or the atmosphere in the home struck Lorraine as unusual. It just seemed like another one of Julie's bad days, nothing more.

Julie, knowing her firearms application had been approved, returned to Lock N Load in Oldmar, arriving at 11:21. She picked up her gun, ammunition, and user's manual. Julie asked questions about how to load and use the firearm while she was there, but Tanso got the impression that she already knew the answers. She was articulate and appeared physically healthy and mentally normal. Once again, she gave no indication to the gun shop staff that there was anything amiss.

Upon returning home, she wrote detailed notes planning the murders of her children and her suicide afterwards.

Calyx saw her IB guidance counselor, Rosanne Hoit, on Thursday to talk about boarding school. "Will you write recommendations for me?" Calyx asked.

"I'll need a complete list of your extracurricular activities to do that. Can you get that to me right away?"

"I'll bring it tomorrow," she said.

After school, Calyx attended track practice. Her mother picked her up and brought her home. Calyx went upstairs to the den, booted up the computer, and signed on to her Facebook page at about four thirty that afternoon. She chatted with her good friend Jena until a few minutes after five thirty. They talked about school, for the most part. Calyx did not say anything about a conflict at her home. She didn't even mention her family. Nothing in their conversation foreshadowed the events that were about to unfold.

The two girls signed off expecting to see each other soon.

It was the night of the friends' weekly ritual of watching *The Office* together. Usually, Sara, Jena, Tatiana, and Calyx all gathered round their webcams, chatting and giggling throughout the show.

It was a cool Tampa winter day with the highs reaching only into the mid-sixties. Julie backed the family mini-van out of the garage and drove through her well-landscaped neighborhood. In the passenger seat, Beau, wearing a sweatshirt and pants, was ready for his soccer practice scheduled to begin in a few minutes, at 7:00 that evening.

Before reaching their destination, Beau said something that set off his clearly unstable mother. She pulled out her new gun and fired a shot into the windshield, making a loud noise in the small space that terrified her son.

It was not clear what the young boy could have said to trigger such a violent reaction from his parent. It is doubtful that his comment was that far out of line.

The reason Julie had her weapon with her in the car is also unclear. Did she plan to store the gun in the car? Did she bring it along simply because it was new? Or did she intentionally come armed for the drive to soccer practice because she was looking for an excuse—any excuse—to draw her weapon and fire?

Confusion, fear, bewilderment, and disbelief crowded into Beau's shocked mind. No one will ever know what thoughts tumbled through his consciousness as he struggled to understand what was happening. Apparently, he believed that his mother was still capable of listening to reason. He pleaded with her, "Mom, put the gun away."

Instead of jolting his mother up out of her strange, inexplicable state, this request fired up Julie's anger even more. She raised the gun and aimed straight at her only son. Beau had only a moment to contemplate his mother's betrayal.

Julie pulled the trigger and sent the lethal projectile through his left temple. Then she fired a second time. That bullet penetrated into his skull, entering through the side of his left nostril, ensuring that he was dead.

She turned around the car and headed back home, the loveable, spirited Beau sprawled lifelessly in the seat beside her. Blood drained from his head and trickled from his mouth.

Julie was not done. She pulled into the garage and walked into her home. She had a daughter whom she'd called mouthy and disrespectful. She had to address that problem in her life, too. She climbed the eighteen steps to the second floor.

CHAPTER 21

Calyx, wearing an orange Florida High School Athletic Association T-shirt and green shorts with white stripes, sat in a rolling office chair in the family den. She was focused on a laptop computer at the wooden workstation. A bookcase stood next to that desk, and against the opposite wall was a futon with a white mattress, white comforter, and two throw pillows. At right angles, a sofa sat beside two file cabinets.

Engrossed in her work, Calyx heard the noise echoing from downstairs as the garage door rose in its tracks, the car pulled inside, and the large door descended to the floor and locked. She was aware of the sounds her mother made as she reentered the family home but paid them little mind. It did not disturb Calyx or disrupt her concentration much at all. She listened as her mother's footsteps came up to the second floor. It's possible that Calyx had a passing hope that her mother would see that she was busy with her schoolwork and walk away, leaving her in peace. She did not want another conflict. She certainly was not concerned enough about her mother's presence to turn around and give her a glance.

Julie saw nothing in that room but her sixteen-year-old daughter. Her anger congealed into action. She stared at the young girl's back and raised her weapon. Unlike Beau,

Calyx did not have any indication that her mother was now totally and irrevocably out of control.

Julie fired her new revolver, shooting her daughter in the back of the head. In a reflexive action, the impact sent Calyx's head to the side. Julie pulled the trigger again. This time, she shot Calyx in the face, just below her mouth.

Julie watched life flee from the body that she had nourished inside her for nine months, sixteen years earlier. Did she feel any remorse? Did she have any regrets? Her actions after this second murder indicate that she did.

Pulling the chair, holding the bleeding body of Calyx away from the desk, Julie rolled it off the plastic floor protector, covered with coarse, medium, and fine spatter. She pushed the burden down the hallway to her teenage daughter's bedroom. In Julie's wake, a double-track trail of blood marked the path she had taken.

Julie lifted her child's body and laid it flat on the bed. She took care to place Calyx's ravaged head partially on a pillow, at the top of the bed. Julie went to the linen closet in the bathroom and grabbed a few towels. She wedged them against her daughter's shoulder to absorb some of the blood. She returned to the closet and retrieved a blanket. Back in Calyx's bedroom, she draped it over the bloodied body of her first-born child.

Julie rolled the desk chair to the den and pushed it snugly into the niche under the workstation, as if tidying up after her children. She went back to the bathroom once again and grabbed a white blanket from the linen closet. Turning off the lights on the second floor, she went back downstairs and into the garage. She opened the front passenger door of the mini-van and removed Beau's bloodstained glasses from his face, propping them on the dashboard. Then she spread out the second blanket, too, covering Beau's body, concealing what she had done to her youngest child.

Although the postmortem covering of her victims indicated that Julie felt a great deal of conflict over what she had done and that she still had a strong feeling of connection to her children, her next act belied those emotions. Julie picked up a Toshiba laptop and sat down in the living room to compose an e-mail message to her husband, Parker: "Get home soon—we're waiting for you!"

CHAPTER 22

Although it is easy to see a dark, malicious intent contained in the e-mail to her husband, it was also possible to wonder if she had entered an extreme state of denial. Her stability had been suspect for more than a year. Had her mind now traveled to a place where reality was unknown? Or did she revel in the fact that she had accomplished her mission to teach her children a lesson?

She reinforced the believability of the possibility that she was totally delusional and disconnected from the real world when a short time later she sent Parker another message: "calyx has all b's and a's=yipps i beau has 2 c's wehich will cross out a couple a's he has, bur till a 3." Was that missive merely an attempt to disarm her husband? Or was it further proof that she had no conscious awareness of her actions?

One can only assume that Parker, like Julie's brother, Dave, had grown accustomed to poor spelling, no capitalization, and awkwardly worded e-mails from his wife. If so, the communication probably raised no alarm, simply a sense of relief that he would be home soon.

Julie sent an e-mail to her mother and siblings that night, too. That message contained a distressing indication that Julie was contemplating suicide. She wrote that she was tired of the kids talking back and added "it would all be over soon." She did not mention the deaths of the two young teenagers in her care. She did not express any remorse for the horrific act she had just completed. No one in the family saw the e-mail until the following morning.

After sending that message, Julie went outside and sat in the lounge chair by the pool, where she chain-smoked and wrote down the details of what she had done and why she had done it. She detailed the shooting of her children and wrote about the next step she planned to take—the one that would end her own life.

According to police reports, her descriptions of her actions were the methodical, nonemotional retelling of the murders of her own children. She wrote about it all in a very matter-of-fact tone.

She picked up her phone after midnight and sent out text messages to Lisa Prisco filled with incoherent abbreviations, jumbled words, and misspellings. One read: "Txt me f or still awake. The hekks r k Comein the mbdoorzthimay be asleep butill be awack—r illbe wacke wjheack when come thru." Half an hour later, she sent another text: "Might need some help this wknd come thru the mb slider—tell me ur are coming k?"

At some point, Julie rose from that chair. Did she simply walk a few steps away and collapse onto the apron of the pool? Or did she make a tour of the home, surveying the consequences of her actions?

CHAPTER 23

Thursday evening, Sara, Jena, and Tatiana jumped on their computers to watch *The Office*. Calyx did not join them. The others were disappointed but not worried. They thought that she either had fallen asleep or had to go out to dinner with her family. That evening, they did not give it another thought.

Julie's parents, Jim and Pat Powers, were beginning another day in Texas, escaping the harsh midwestern winter in the warmer southern state. On January 28, 2011, Pat checked her e-mail. What she found shook her hard. The message from her daughter made Julie's current state of severe depression glaringly obvious. Her complaints about her children and her ominous statement that "it would all be over soon" rocked Pat to her core.

She tried to call her daughter Julie but got no answer. Pat dialed the cell phones of both Beau and Calyx, but neither of them picked up. Something was not right. Pat wanted to rush over there and check on the family herself, but she was too far away. Helpless to take direct action, she looked up the number for the police in Tampa and dialed it with shaking hands. She explained the situation in her daughter's North Tampa home and asked them to please go to the

Schenecker house and make sure that all was well with her daughter and grandchildren.

Officer William Copulos received a message from Dispatch informing him of the need to make a welfare check at a home where a mother might be suicidal and the two children, suspected of being the only other two residents in the house, were not responding to phone calls.

He and Officer Gregory Noble entered the upscale gated community using the code that every secured community is required by law to provide to police and emergency services.

The Schenecker home was a two-story, concrete-block, thirty-three-hundred-square-foot single-family residence. The house was tan trimmed in white, with the house numbers affixed above the garage door. The entry doors faced west and, like the rest of the trim, were painted white. Cement pavers extended from the garage to the street.

When no one answered the front door, Officers Noble and Cupolos walked into the sixty-by-one-hundred-foot backyard. They opened one of the two doors from the lawn to the screened enclosure around the cement-marcite swimming pool, where they discovered Julie, lying on the back porch, upon the hard surface of the pool apron rather than the far more comfortable white vinyl outdoor lounger.

They scanned the area with trained eyes with every step they took. Scattered around the pool were various pool chemicals and cleansers. Next to a green pool float officers found three cigarette butts. Beyond that were another inflated float, a round beach ball, and an assortment of other deflated pool toys.

From inside the enclosure, entry to the house was accessible through two sets of sliding doors—one into the family room, the other into the master bedroom. On a window ledge beside the latter an empty, clear water bottle sat beside an ashtray overflowing with dozens of cigarette butts, a crumpled green cigarette box, a pair of red-handled garden flower clippers, and a *Real Simple* magazine opened to an article titled "9 Easy Ways to Be Happier."

Beside the main entrance into the house were a hockey

stick, two pairs of flip-flops, and a pair of orange Croc slide-on shoes. The officers absorbed these surroundings in a matter of seconds, registering the typical dishevelment of a busy family home. They turned their attention to the semi-conscious woman lying at their feet. The sight of her wiped all thoughts of normalcy out of their minds. The woman, presumed to be Julie Schenecker, wore a bathrobe spattered with blood—lots of blood. Her face was speckled with even more of it, and they could also discern a fine black powder dusting her features.

When Julie agreed to their request to go into the house and check on the children, the officers escorted her inside and into the family room. Next to the family room was the formal living room still decked out for Christmas, complete with un-opened, prettily wrapped packages. In her chaotic emotional state, Julie apparently neglected to ship or hand-deliver some of the gifts the family had purchased.

Past the tree, a pair of French doors with a dead bolt and lever handle led to a foyer. The lock was not fastened and was intact. Next was a formal dining room with a wooden table, five chairs, and a cabinet, its drawers filled with silverware. Next to the cabinet was a coatrack and beside that a piece of furniture containing dinnerware.

On top of the dining table was a white clothes basket filled with folded shorts, socks, boxer underwear, and shirts. Directly on the surface were a neat stack of towels and a pair of green-and-blue plaid pajama bottoms. Nothing there looked at all unusual.

Copulos led Julie into the kitchen, situated between the dining room and the family room, where chicken and an opened container of blueberry yogurt sat unrefrigerated on the counter next to stacks of mail and magazines. A small crate of clementines, some oranges, a bowl filled with plums, and another with vegetables sat nearby.

The sink was littered with items that needed cleaning, including two plates, a pot, and a fork. Next to it sat an empty, used wineglass and an assortment of utensils. A cutting board holding a serving bowl with chicken at least a day old rested on the center island. On a white plate beside it was a piece of chicken with a fork and a yellow Post-it note that read: "Calyx wouldn't eat the French chicken. Was going to make something else??" Although that note was not threatening, it was foreboding under the current unknown circumstances.

In the garbage can in the cabinet under the center island, unseen by the officers, were three empty Heineken beer bottles and a two discarded wine bottles, one of which once held Vendange Chardonnay, the other Vendange Merlot, as well as soda cans and other refuse.

A brown purse sat on another counter. Inside it, a receipt dated January 22, 2011, for a .38-caliber Smith & Wesson Bodyguard handgun and a box of ammunition from Lock N Load in Oldsmar, Florida. That was certainly a red flag.

Officer Noble was intent on his mission to locate Calyx and Beau. In the master bedroom he spotted another laundry basket, partially filled with clothing, on the floor next to a chest of drawers. The bed was disheveled, with the comforter and top sheet tangled on the floor at the foot of the mattress. In the middle of the bed he found a prescription bottle with twelve small pills. The label bore Julie's name and identified the contents as clonazepam, a long-acting muscle relaxer and hypnotic used for anxiety and as a secondary epilepsy drug, known for causing drowsiness and cognitive impairment. Even after use has ended, this drug caused memory loss that could be permanent. "Sleep" was scrawled in handwriting across it. Next to it was a black cell phone, a flower-topped green ink pen, and a blue spiral notebook, later discovered to be full of the incriminating commentary regarding Julie's deadly plans and the actual commission of a double homicide.

On one of the nightstands flanking the bed, a turned-on lamp revealed an empty Heineken beer can and a bottle, emptied of its contents—its label marking it as once containing hydrocodone, a narcotic analgesic, prescribed to relieve pain and coughing—in contrast to the clonazepam, it was known for causing anxiety.

Labels on other bottles revealed the presence of more serious and often unpredictable pharmaceuticals: benzatropine, used to reduce the side effects of antipsychotic drugs and to treat Parkinson's disease but, taken in excess, having the capability of inducing psychosis: lithium, prescribed to prevent episodes of mania in people with bipolar disorder, its long list of potential side effects included depression, joint and muscle pain, tiredness, weakness and twitching of the muscles, slow, jerky movements, and blackouts; and oxycodone—now depleted of pills—a narcotic pain reliever derived from synthetic opium, which often brought on memory loss, fatigue, and anxiety. All of the labels bore Julie Schenecker's name—a troubling combination of drugs that indicated there were serious problems in this woman's life.

Inside the top drawer of the small table was another bottle labeled "Lithium" as well as one for amoxicillin, an antibiotic, and a third, now-empty bottle, for triazolam, a sleeping pill—also prescribed for Julie. Noble found a handgun on the dresser and secured it.

Then he discovered the box of ammunition in the bathroom. On the vanity next to that he spotted five empty shell casings, a business card for Colonel Parker Schenecker, "USA Deputy NSA/CSS, Representative," a man's gold wedding band, and six more prescription bottles for Julie Schenecker: venlafaxin-hydrochloride and citalopram, both antidepressants; warfarin and coumadin, two anticoagulant drugs; buspirone, an antianxiety medication; lamotrigine, used to treat epileptic seizures; and a white prescription bag with seven loose pills.

On the second floor of the home Officer Noble spotted a large quantity of dried, spilled blood around the desk. He followed the trail of dark red that led from there to a closed bedroom door, apprehension increasing with every step he took. Opening it, he found the body of Calyx, covered with a blanket, on top of her bed. The bloodied face of the young girl sickened him. He checked to make sure she was deceased and then checked the other bedroom and bath, hoping to find Beau alive and hiding somewhere in the house.

Everywhere Officer Noble went, he spotted Post-it notes. One read: "Do not resuscitate." He had no idea if that message referred to the children or if it was a note written by Julie in reference to herself, as the suicidal e-mail to her family indicated was a possibility. Either way, the message was as dark and disturbing as a swamp on a moonless night.

Back downstairs, he went down a hall, past the laundry room, and into a three-car garage, where a chalkboard hanging on the wall bore the mind-boggling message: "2011, Best Year ever." Inside was a black Volkswagen Passat and a white Honda Odyssey mini-van. Noble's hopes were dashed by his next ominous discovery: a single bullet hole, shot from the inside out, marring the windshield of the Honda. Inside he found the sight he dreaded: young Beau, sitting in the passenger side, covered with a blanket, dead from multiple gunshot wounds to the head. Even with the evidence right before the officer's eyes, it was difficult to believe that any mother in this upscale community could brutally shoot both of her children.

After being read her Miranda rights, Julie confirmed the reality, confessing to shooting her son twice in the head on the way to soccer practice. She then admitted she drove home and shot Calyx in the back of the head while her daughter was studying.

What Julie told the officers confirmed the suspicions arising from the destruction and death they viewed upstairs and in the garage. The only time she grew emotional, however, was when she learned that she was going to go to jail.

CHAPTER 24

Sergeant Preyer called the station to request the presence of his supervisor Lieutenant Diane Hobley-Burney, the commanding officer for all District Two police ranked at sergeant or below. He did not summon Fire Rescue—he knew it was too late for them to render aid.

In response, he received a call informing him that the homicide squad had been contacted and detectives were on the way. With the arrival of additional patrol backup, Preyer had officers secure the exterior of the home and then stationed one at each of the doors—front and back. Copulos escorted the cuffed suspect out to his car and secured her in the backseat. She shook uncontrollably and her eyes looked as if she had just survived a violent attack.

Detective Gary Sandel arrived on the scene just after eight thirty that morning. On the way into the house, he spotted Julie Schenecker sitting in the backseat of a patrol car. After a briefing from Sergeant Preyer, Sandel directed Copulos to transport Julie Schenecker to police headquarters at 411 North Franklin Street. Sandel then called Detective Michael Kirlangitis and asked him to write a search warrant. After that, the detective walked the perimeter of the house examining all the first-floor windows and doors for any indications of a forced entry. He found none.

Copulos arrived at the station house with the prisoner

and briefed Detective Kirlangitis on the situation they found at the Schenecker home. He then waited with Julie in the eighth-floor holding cell until he was relieved.

Detective Sandel left the crime scene, traveling to headquarters to interview the woman in custody. At his request, Officer Sonya McCaughey relieved Copulos, sitting down with the suspect in the confined space at 10:20 that morning. Julie was still wearing pajamas, slippers, and a robe, but the belt had been removed from her waist and placed outside of the cell.

McCaughey offered Julie water, cookies, and coffee with cream and sugar. While drinking the water, Julie slipped into sleep, causing the liquid to spill on her clothing. McCaughey reached for the bottle and Julie woke up. She pressed the bottle to her lips again, but as soon as she started drinking she had a coughing spell.

"Is the water too cold?" McCaughey asked.

"It just went down the wrong pipe," Julie answered.

Sandel contacted Detective Stephen Prebich, requesting photographs and the recovery of Julie's clothing as evidence. A crime scene technician entered the cell to photograph and retrieve the clothing worn by the prisoner. The tech brought along a white bio-suit with a jacket and booties to replace Julie's personal garments.

Following directions from Detective Sandel, the tech photographed the splatter on Julie's face, the fine black powder on her left cheek, and the deep red stains on her hands, clothing, and accessories. The handcuffs were removed from Julie's wrists, and the bloodied watch from her left wrist was confiscated and placed into a marked bag as evidence.

Next, her robe and slippers were removed and each secured in a separate container. Her bloodstained pants came off next. Seeing that Julie wore no underwear, police officers were considerate enough to pull the pants of the bio-suit up to her waist before her pajama top was taken off to be replaced by the jacket of the suit. The tech pulled booties on Julie's feet. The two pieces of her pajamas were secured in individual bags. Julie was then escorted to the conference room for an interview.

She told the detectives that she shot Beau because he had been "talking back." She said that Calyx was "mouthy."

After questioning the suspect, Detective Sandel contacted the state attorney's office and reiterated the substance of the interview. Investigators Sandel and Prebish completed an affidavit and charged Julie with two counts of first-degree murder. Kiriangitis obtained a judge's signature on the search warrant and read the document to Julie, who still appeared as dazed as she was when Officers Copulos and Noble found her at her home.

Every three days, somewhere in this country, a mother kills her child. It is a crime that runs contrary to all intuitive expectations regarding the mother-child bond. Law enforcement now knew that Julie Schenecker was one of that number—but knowing that did not answer the biggest question: Why?

CHAPTER 25

At lunchtime in the high school cafeteria, Jena was concerned that Calyx was not in school and her worry was heightened when she realized that no one had heard from Calyx since yesterday when she chatted with her on Facebook.

Jena sent Calyx a text: "WHERE ARE YOU?"

She received no response.

Back on Royal Park Court, Detective Ruth Cato arrived on the scene to assist the homicide squad. Sergeant Mark Delage lifted the yellow crime scene tape that blocked off the street to allow Cato to drive up the road to the house. She parked by the curb and was still in the front yard being briefed by Detective Eric Houston when a vehicle backed out of a neighbor's residence.

"Go talk to that woman," Detective Houston told Cato. "Ask what kind of person Julie is."

Cato walked up to the vehicle, which stopped as she approached. The woman inside introduced herself as Pamela Elsaadi. "Will you speak to me?" Cato asked.

"Certainly," Pamela said as she nodded.

"Are you friends with Julie?"

"You really should speak to Julie's best friends, Lisa Prisco and Lorraine Livingston. I've had dinner with Julie and Parker and seen them at other house parties, but I have never had any one-on-one time with Julie or chatted with her on the telephone."

"When was the last time you saw Julie?" Cato asked.

"Well, I saw her this morning being escorted out of the house by the police."

"Do you know Julie's closest friends?"

"Yes," Pamela answered. "I am friends with Lisa Prisco and Lorraine Livingston. I spoke to both of them this morning. Lisa said that Julie sent her a text message at around one a.m. I don't know exactly what it said. Lorraine called, too, because when she drove past Julie's house and when she saw the police she wanted to know what was going on."

"Do you know how I can reach these women?"

"Lorraine is leaving for New York today, but you can call her cell phone," Pamela said, providing that number as well as Lisa's number to Cato. "Lisa lives on the next cul-de-sac off of Sambourne."

"Could you describe Julie?" the officer asked.

"Julie is nice, shy, not too outgoing. I don't think she works. She's had a lot of problems lately and was recently hospitalized at a drug treatment program in Clearwater for prescription drugs."

"How long was she there?"

"May have been a month," Pamela said.

"When's the last time you saw the kids?"

Pamela's brow furrowed. She shook her head and said, "I don't know."

"Have you ever seen the kids?"

"Yes. Julie's son plays with the Zahrobsky boy. I don't have any kids that age, but I think he must be around nine to eleven years old. I know they have a daughter, but she's a teenager and I don't see her much. Julie's husband is in the military. He left for Afghanistan two weeks ago."

"Have you ever been inside?" Cato asked, jerking her head toward the Schenecker residence.

"No," Pamela said.

"Did you hear anything strange from Julie's house last night?"

"No," the neighbor said with a shake of her head. "I went to sleep around nine or nine thirty last night."

"Do you live in the house alone?"

"No. I live with my husband, Nibal Elsaadi."

"Where was he last night?"

"He was at home with me."

"Is there anything else I should know?" Cato asked.

"I think there is a conflict between Julie and her daughter."

"What makes you say that?"

"I've heard them arguing—but not last night."

"Arguing about what?"

"Just mother-daughter friction, I think."

CHAPTER 26

Officer Cato continued her interviews by placing a call to Lorraine Livingston, who was at the airport awaiting her flight to New York. After identifying herself, Cato asked Lorraine how she knew Julie.

"I used to live in the same neighborhood," Lorraine said.

"How would you describe your relationship?"

"She's one of my best friends—we're all girlfriends; we go out together. Are the kids okay?"

"We'll talk about that later," Cato said, and then asked, "What was Julie's relationship like with her kids?"

"They are all going to counseling."

"Why?"

Lorraine pulled back, feeling protective of the family. "I can't go into detail, but the mother and teenager have arguments every now and then."

"When was the last time you saw Julie?"

"I haven't seen her for two months," Lorraine said, a statement that she has since contradicted.

"Why not?" Cato asked.

"Because the family is going through some changes," Lorraine answered, continuing to be vague.

"When did you last talk to Julie?"

"Last week on the phone. Julie said, 'You know, Lorraine, we are going to counseling. We are trying.'"

"Do you know where Julie's husband is?"

"Yes. Parker is in Afghanistan."

"Do you know anything about the Post-it notes found on the Scheneckers' front door this morning?"

"I know I didn't put them there," Lorraine said. "I was on the way to Julie's to borrow a pair of boots for my trip. I saw the police there and they wouldn't let me go up to the house. They told me Julie was okay but did not mention the kids. Are they okay?"

Cato thanked Lorraine and ended the call, leaving Lorraine's desperate question unanswered.

CHAPTER 27

After her interview with Lorraine Livingston, Officer Cato contacted Detective Danny Rhodes. Together they made the short trip to Sambourne Lane to speak to Julie's other good friend, Lisa Prisco, and her husband, John.

"I haven't seen Julie this week," Lisa said. "But I did talk to her a few days ago."

"When did you last see her?" Rhodes asked.

"I think the last time I actually *saw* her was in September."

"You're close friends, you live nearby, why haven't you seen her since then?"

"Julie went away to a rehab center in Safety Harbor."

"What was wrong with Julie?" Cato asked.

Lisa, just like Lorraine, put up a wall against that personal question, reluctant to reveal the truth about her friend's condition, as if sensing it would be a betrayal.

John interrupted, "Lisa, just tell the officer what is going on."

Lisa looked at her husband, then back at her questioners. "The family was in counseling. They've been in counseling since the fall. Julie was currently in the care of a military doctor—maybe for depression and being bipolar. Her medication is not meshing."

"What do you mean?" Cato asked.

"Julie is forgetful. We'd be having a conversation and

Julie would forget what she was saying or what she had just said. She would forget what she did the night before. I told her to jot down notes to help remember and tell the doctor about her forgetfulness." Lisa sighed. "The family is having a lot of problems and I kept pushing them to go into therapy. Julie told me they were going to counseling, but Julie complained a lot about the counselor and her inability to remember things because of her medications."

"Do you know what she was taking?"

"Her normal doctor has her on about a dozen different medications and the doctor she saw for injuries in her car accident prescribed percocet and hydrocodone, which I think is against the regular doctor's orders. Now Julie has tardive dyskinesia."

"What is that?" Cato asked.

"It's because she's been taking her medications for too long. Because of that, Julie can't control herself physically—her legs jerk and her arms twitch."

"How do you know Julie?"

"I met her four years ago when I was her real estate agent. I moved them into their house, and we've been best friends ever since."

"Who lives at the house?"

"Julie, Parker, Calyx, who is sixteen, Beau, who's thirteen, and two cats."

"What do you know about the children?"

"They're both good students. Calyx is very driven academically. She wants to be a doctor. She gets all A's and is in the IB Program at King High School. But she's about to go off to a boarding school."

"Why?" Cato asked.

"Calyx doesn't want to live in the house."

"How long has that been going on?"

"Since before Christmas. Calyx stopped speaking to Julie. Julie complained that Calyx would not answer her questions. Parker was trying to get Calyx into a good school before he deployed. I think he finished the paperwork and it's probably sitting on the kitchen counter. But Parker just left for Afghanistan."

"Do you know anything about the relationship between Julie and Parker?"

"They've been married for twenty years—I think they met in college, but I'm not sure. Parker has been trying to do what a dad can do. All of the fighting between Julie and Calyx has been too much for him."

"What about Beau? What do you know about him?"

Lisa laughed softly. "He is so-o-o funny. He plays soccer—he's always playing at the front court with other kids in the neighborhood."

Officer Cato turned the interview back to a previous line of questioning: "If Julie is your best friend and she just lives down the street, why has it been so long since you have seen her?"

"Last month was a difficult month for us. My father-in-law passed away and we went to New Jersey. Then the holidays and this month, I've been sick with the flu. Julie has been asking me to come over, but I didn't want to get them sick so I didn't go."

"What was the source of all the arguing between Calyx and her mother?"

"Julie said that Calyx would tell her: 'You're not my mother.' Other than that, she just wasn't speaking to Julie. When Julie cooked, Calyx would take her plate and go eat in her room. Calyx complained, 'My mom is a terrible cook. I won't eat foods out of a box. I want everything to be green.' But everything was fine at Thanksgiving."

"That was two years ago, Lisa," John interjected.

"Oh, right. I met both of the mothers then. Parker's mother is Nancy Schenecker and she lives in New York. I think Julie's mom lives in New Orleans. They're all friends on Facebook." Lisa pulled up the pages on Facebook and then showed them a recent post by Parker from the Middle East and the postings on Beau's page.

"What do you know about Parker?"

"He works with Intelligence and I think he's a general. Julie was in the military, too. She was a Russian interrogator."

"Is there anything else that could help us?" Cato asked.

"A couple of months ago, Julie slapped Calyx and DCF [Department of Children & Families] came."

"Do either of you know if there are any guns in the house?" Cato asked Lisa and John.

"No way would Parker leave a gun in the house with all that was going on," John said.

"Do you know if Julie had bought a gun?"

"No," John and Lisa said in unison.

Lisa continued, "How about the children? How are the children?"

"I'll come back and give you an update," Cato promised. She left the Prisco home and soon learned that the media were about to report that two bodies had been found in the Schenecker house. She and Detective Rhodes went back to see John and Lisa, telling them that both of the children were dead.

Distraught, Lisa sobbed and said, "No, no, no," over and over.

John tried to comfort his wife, but she was inconsolable. He turned to Cato. "I just can't understand why a gun was in the house," he said, then swallowed hard and closed his eyes. When he reopened them, he added, "If you need me to identify the bodies, I will since no immediate family is available right now."

Lisa said that she'd received text messages from Julie last night but did not see them until this morning. "Julie never texts me that late. I saw them this morning and tried to call her at eight, but she didn't answer her phone." Lisa allowed Rhodes to photograph the messages on her cell phone and then forwarded them to Cato's e-mail.

That day in Qatar, Parker was informed by U.S. Army personnel that his wife had killed their children.

CHAPTER 28

Officer Cato next went to the C. Leon King High School, where Calyx was enrolled. Cato spoke to Principal Carla Bruning, SRO Deputy Johnson, Assistant Principal Yinka Alege, IB assistant principal Matt Romano, IB guidance counselor Rosanna Hoit, and school psychologist Etta Rahming. None of them knew of any problems being reported by Calyx.

"I saw her yesterday," Hoit said. "We discussed preparing a recommendation to boarding school. She was going to provide me with more information."

Cato requested a copy of Calyx's class schedule and Alege provided it.

The officer asked him, "When was the last time Calyx was in school?"

"Yesterday," he said. "Actually, today was Calyx's first absence all school year and she'd only been tardy once back in November."

Mainly through text messages, word of the tragedy spread through King High School like a flash flood, stunning students up and down every corridor. Coach Gary Bingham wanted to gather his team together to deliver the news to all of them as a group, but before he could do it they already knew. At the end of the day, he was busy making car-pool arrangements for the team members who had driven themselves to school and were now too distraught to get behind the wheel for the ride home.

One by one, the Ostuaries learned of Calyx's death. After school, one of Sara's friends said, "I learned something that I need to tell you."

She looked at him and knew something was wrong. "Yes?" she said.

He then told her what happened to Calyx the day before. Sara did not want to believe what she heard.

Jena heard about it on the way home from school from another student in her car pool.

Tatiana was out sick from school that day. She remained in her Apollo Beach home on a canal that, after a few twists and turns, led out to Tampa Bay. She was sitting on her mom's bed when her mother, Latanya, answered the phone and began to cry. "It can't be," she wailed to the person on the other end of the line.

When she disconnected from the call, Tatiana asked, "Mom, what?"

Latanya pulled Tatiana close, "I don't know how to tell you this. . . ." And then she told her about Calyx and Beau, and Tatiana's world went into a tailspin.

Late that afternoon, the moms of the Ostuaries, along with their daughters, gathered together at Sara's house to make a poster for the vigil that night. On it was a quotation by Albus Dumbledore—Harry Potter's headmaster: "To the well-organized mind, death is but the next great adventure."

In Texas that afternoon, Julie's high school friend Sylvia Carroll, who had reignited her old friendship with Julie a couple of years earlier, was sitting down, relaxing and watching Oprah acknowledging military folks and the families left at home. While the show was rolling, Sylvia checked her Facebook and saw a message from a resourceful Associated Press reporter, who had used the social network to track down Julie's friends: "Sorry to hear about the tragedy with your high school friend Julie."

What does that mean? Sylvia wondered. *Has Julie died?* It was hard to imagine that the fit, athletic woman could have succumbed to any illness. An accident? Sylvia searched the Internet and found the photo taken of her friend after her arrest. No. That could not be the Julie Powers she knew in high school. It looked like a psycho woman. But there she was. The same last name Sylvia had used to find her old friend on Facebook. Sylvia felt as if part of her youth, her innocence, had imploded.

Out on the West Coast, Julie's Hawaiian roommate, Darcelle, was on a layover in Seattle. On the television mounted above her she saw something on the news about someone killing her kids for being mouthy. Darcelle turned from her TV and looked back at her e-mail and switched over to news on the Internet.

She found the photo of the woman in the news and thought, *I know someone who looks like that. What a coincidence.* The woman in the story was named Julie and that was Darcelle's roommate's name, too. And her last name looked something like that of the woman in the picture. But it couldn't be the same Julie Darcelle knew. Those two delightful children could not be dead.

Although it had been a dozen years since Darcelle witnessed her own sister's demise, the murders of Calyx and Beau burrowed into the fault lines left in her heart from the earlier tragedy. Their deaths resurrected Darcelle's old pain and added a layer of new agony.

Julie's neighbor clinical psychologist Tsila Abush Kirsh left the neighborhood Friday morning at seven. She went to her son's school to volunteer. A neighbor approached her and asked, "Have you heard what's happening in the neighborhood?"

"No, what happened?"

"The police are there. They blocked the road, but I don't know what's happening," the neighbor said.

"It must have been murder if the road is blocked."

That afternoon, she learned what happened at the Schenecker home from a student at Liberty Middle School. Even though the school day ended before any adults could address the situation with the children, the kids knew by text messages and hallway chatter. Being a mental health professional did not protect Kirsh from being traumatized—she was shocked and incredulous at what had happened.

Returning home, she encountered emotional upheaval in her neighborhood: "All in all, though, I was very proud of my community—very proud—the way they pulled together so quickly in the immediate aftermath and got things together for each other with great speed."

The news of the Schenecker tragedy drifted down the streets of the Ashleigh Reserve development, leaking its infectious poison through the doorsills of each home, shattering the established perception of reality at every house.

Even if the neighbors did not know any of the family members, even if they'd never even heard the Schenecker name, it was now on all of their lips and burrowing deep into their minds. The psyche's natural refuge of denial whispered, then shouted, *It can't happen here.* And yet it did. A community's innocence was lost. The false sense of security of life in a gated neighborhood was exposed to be as mocking a sham as the emperor's new clothes.

On a counter in the master bathroom, police found an opened box of ammunition and spent shells used to shoot Calyx and Beau Schenecker (Courtesy of the Office of the State Attorney, 13th Judicial Court, Hillsborough County)

The rear of the Schneckers' home with the attached pool area where police found Julie Schenecker sleeping on the concrete apron on the morning of January 28, 2011. (Courtesy of the Office of the State Attorney, 13th Judicial Court, Hillsborough County)

After finding the body of Calyx Schenecker, police entered the bedroom of her younger brother Beau, where police feared they would find another dead body. But Beau's bed was empty. (Courtesy of the Office of the State Attorney, 13th Judicial Court, Hillsborough County)

A drum set sat silently against the wall of Beau's bedroom, never to be played by him again. (Courtesy of the Office of the State Attorney, 13th Judicial Court, Hillsborough County)

Julie fired a bullet through the windshield before turning the gun on Beau. His bloodied glasses flew off his face and onto the dashboard. (Courtesy of the Office of the State Attorney, 13th Judicial Court, Hillsborough County)

Calyx Schenecker

Relay For Life Team Captain
Wizarding Independence Day

At the request of her team, Calyx will remain the captain of Wizarding Independence Day, as they raise awareness of and money for the programs and services of the American Cancer Society.

At the request of the students who chair this event, which will bring together over 650 King High School students on March 19-20, the 2011 Relay For Life at King High School will be dedicated to the memory of Calyx.

You can honor her memory by helping to make Calyx the top fundraiser. Visit www.relayforlife.org/kinghsfl and click on her team name, and then on her name, to make a donation.

Announcement posted regarding the American Cancer Society Relay for Life at King High School. Although the event was scheduled weeks after Calyx's death, her team members voted to continue with Calyx as the official team captain.

The bed in Calyx's bedroom where Julie Schenecker had placed the body of her deceased child. (Courtesy of the Office of the State Attorney, 13th Judicial Court, Hillsborough County)

The blood spatter on the carpet and acrylic floor protector beneath the chair where Calyx had been sitting when her mother pulled the trigger and shot her in the head. (Courtesy of the Office of the State Attorney, 13th Judicial Court, Hillsborough County)

The Christmas tree with wrapped presents beneath the branches still stood in the Schenecker living room more than a month after the holiday. (Courtesy of the Office of the State Attorney, 13th Judicial Court, Hillsborough County)

A detective and a forensic specialist examine Julie and Parker's marital bed where bottles of prescription medicines were found. (Courtesy of the Office of the State Attorney, 13th Judicial Court, Hillsborough County)

In the living room of the Schenecker home, shelves filled with family photographs recall happier moments in the lives of the family. (Courtesy of the Office of the State Attorney, 13th Judicial Court, Hillsborough County)

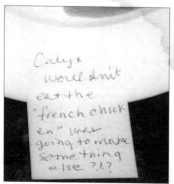

A dried plate of food sat on the kitchen counter with a Post-It note, in Julie's handwriting, that read: "Calyx wouldn't eat the 'french chicken' was going to make something else??" (Courtesy of the Office of the State Attorney, 13th Judicial Court, Hillsborough County)

A member of law enforcement examines the screen door leading from the outside into the pool area behind the Schenecker home. (Courtesy of the Office of the State Attorney, 13th Judicial Court, Hillsborough County)

A receipt from the Lock N Load gun store in Florida, showing the details of Julie's purchase of the Smith and Wesson handgun and ammunition. (Courtesy of the Office of the State Attorney, 13th Judicial Court, Hillsborough County)

Parker, Julie, Calyx and Beau smile in a family portrait sitting on a table in the master bedroom of the Schenecker home. (Courtesy of the Office of the State Attorney, 13th Judicial Court, Hillsborough County)

The Schenecker home at 16305 Royal Park Court in North Tampa where the bodies of young Calyx and Beau were found with evidence of gunshots in their heads. (Courtesy of the Office of the State Attorney, 13th Judicial Court, Hillsborough County)

The Schenecker family pool, where Julie, Parker, Calyx and Beau enjoyed relaxing and swimming nearly year round. (Courtesy of the Office of the State Attorney, 13th Judicial Court, Hillsborough County)

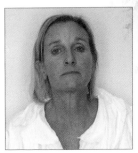

Upon her arrest on January 28, 2011, the Hillsborough County Jail took a photograph of the new prisoner as part of the intake processing procedure. (Courtesy of Hillsborough County Sheriff's Office)

The cluttered kitchen of the Schenecker home. (Courtesy of the Office of the State Attorney, 13th Judicial Court, Hillsborough County)

The disheveled marital bed of Julie and Parker Schenecker where investigators found an extraordinary selection of pharmaceutical prescriptions, a journal and other miscellaneous items. (Courtesy of the Office of the State Attorney, 13th Judicial Court, Hillsborough County)

The .38 caliber Smith and Wesson Body Guard handgun used to shoot and kill Calyx and Beau Schenecker. (Courtesy of the Office of the State Attorney, 13th Judicial Court, Hillsborough County)

Notes taken at the crime scene by law enforcement. (Courtesy of the Office of the State Attorney, 13th Judicial Court, Hillsborough County)

A glimpse into the swimming pool area where Julie Schenecker was found unconscious on the concrete apron. (Courtesy of the Office of the State Attorney, 13th Judicial Court, Hillsborough County)

Although it was more than a month after Christmas, Santa hats still marched up to the second floor of the Schenecker home where 16-year-old Calyx lost her life. (Courtesy of the Office of the State Attorney, 13th Judicial Court, Hillsborough County)

Julie sat to the left on the sofa behind the laptop when she wrote the disturbing email messages to her husband Parker in Kuwait and the garbled notes she sent to her friend up the street. (Courtesy of the Office of the State Attorney, 13th Judicial Court, Hillsborough County)

Julie sat here smoking after killing her children. Ironically, a *Real Simple* magazine was opened to an article entitled "9 Easy Ways to Be Happier." (Courtesy of the Office of the State Attorney, 13th Judicial Court, Hillsborough County)

A forensic technician takes the box for the Smith and Wesson handgun into custody as evidence in the crime. (Courtesy of the Office of the State Attorney, 13th Judicial Court, Hillsborough County)

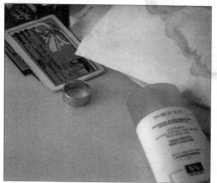

When Parker Schenecker left the country to his deployment in the Middle East, he left behind his wedding band on the counter of the master bathroom. (Courtesy of the Office of the State Attorney, 13th Judicial Court, Hillsborough County)

Calyx Schenecker was sitting in this chair in front of the desk working on her computer when her mother shot her in the back of the head and in her face. (Courtesy of the Office of the State Attorney, 13th Judicial Court, Hillsborough County)

Law enforcement strung up yellow crime scene tape around the swimming pool enclosure behind the Schenecker home. (Courtesy of the Office of the State Attorney, 13th Judicial Court, Hillsborough County)

CHAPTER 29

Those who knew the family or one of the children were hit hardest in the aftermath of the shocking crime. But even those across the entire Tampa Bay area who had never heard of Ashleigh Reserve or had never even seen photographs of North Tampa before the horror filled their televisions, radios, and newspapers were staggered by the story. It was difficult at all times to understand how anyone could murder a child.

Child killers, however, weren't unknown to this seaside region. In the decade before the deaths of Beau and Calyx, the news of such crimes had reverberated through the media and into their lives.

Of the many cases, two garnered widespread attention on the national news front. One was the murder of eleven-year-old Carla Brucia on Super Bowl Sunday in 2004. A video camera at a car wash captured her abduction and riveted attention from coast to coast. Her body was found four days later in a grove of Brazilian pepper trees behind a church.

Joseph Smith was arrested the following day and convicted of her assault, kidnapping, and murder. At his sentencing the judge said, "Her death was conscienceless and pitiless and undoubtedly unnecessarily torturous. The scales of life and death tilt unequivocally on the side of death," and sent him to reside at Union Correctional Institution in Raiford, Florida, in a cell on death row.

The second case was the disappearance of nine-year-old Jessica Lunsford. John Couey, a registered sex offender, kept Jessica alive for three days of sexual assault. He then buried her alive with her purple stuffed dolphin.

Passions in the Tampa Bay area were so inflamed that the judge suspended jury selection after two days because of the difficulty of finding impartial jurors and moved the trial to Miami. After several delays of deliberations, Couey received a death sentence, but he died of colon cancer before the sentence could be executed.

Stranger homicides like those, as horrific as they were, were easier for the public to understand than were deaths as a result of domestic violence committed in the home, by a parent—but that wasn't an unprecedented occurrence in Florida, either. That's just what happened to Patty Para-Perez and her two children, thirteen-year-old Lauren and twelve-year-old Sean. They returned to their home in northwest Hillsborough County on December 10, 2004, where they were ambushed by Robert O'Mara, Patty's ex-husband and the father of the two children. He called out his wife's name; when she turned toward him, he shot Patty in the head. Sean panicked and ran to the front door, desperate to get inside of the house. His father caught up with Sean quickly and shot him, too. Lauren screamed and ran up the street; O'Mara chased her down and fired a shot into her body. O'Mara then put the gun to his own head and pulled the trigger. After a lot of healing and rehabilitation Patty survived, but both of her children were dead.

As dreadful as this triple murder was, it still does not have the same impact as when a mother murders a child. A crime like that makes many people reevaluate the way they view the world, their sense of security, and the sanctity of mother love that society takes for granted. Like Julie Schenecker, two other women with serious mental illness had taken the lives of their own children in the Tampa Bay area in the not-too-distant past.

On January 23, 1990, Dorothy Ross thought she was going to lose custody of her two children, two-year-old Michael and thirteen-month-old Jessica, to her husband and his girl-friend. Dorothy strangled the two toddlers and then slit her own wrists. She was found guilty by reason of insanity and sent to a mental health facility where she still remained twenty-two years later.

Another mother, home health nurse Kristina Gaime, told co-workers that she and her children were all set to go to heaven. No one thought that Kristina meant right away. But on April 12, 1999, soon after they had all returned from a Caribbean cruise, Kristina handed six pills each to her two sons, eight-year-old Adam and six-year-old Matthew. She told them it was aspirin—it was really morphine.

She carried the boys out to the van and connected a hose to the tailpipe. She joined them in the vehicle and turned it on. The next day, she and Adam were found alive, but six-year-old Matthew was dead. In a plea bargain, Kristina received a twenty-year sentence over the objections of her parents, who felt she needed psychiatric treatment rather than prison treatment.

Now another mother in the Tampa Bay area had committed an unspeakable, unbelievable act—with less provocation and more violent intent than anyone could comprehend—and two more innocent children were dead. The question "why?" echoed up and down the streets throughout communities along the Gulf Coast.

CHAPTER 30

Detectives Sandel and Prebich returned to Royal Park Court at 4:32 p.m. and received a walk-through from Detective Henry Duran. Forty-five minutes after their arrival, Medical Examiner Dr. Vernard Adams was ready for the examination of the crime scenes and the viewing of both bodies in situ, a prerequisite before they could be removed from the home.

On his way to the stairway, he glanced at the framed picture of the two victims' smiling faces hanging above a beige sectional sofa—the contrast with what he was about to see was as extreme as any comparison could possibly be. On the second floor, he observed the condition and location of Calyx's body lying on her bed before going back downstairs and into the garage. He first examined Beau through the rolled-down passenger window. He then opened the driver's door and carefully, with Detective Houston's assistance, eased the body out of the car and placed Beau on a sheet stretched out flat on the garage floor.

There Adams leaned over Beau and examined his injuries more closely. When Adams was satisfied that he had seen all he needed to see at the scene, the two young victims were loaded into medical examiner transport units. They pulled out of the driveway taking Calyx and Beau away from the home for the last time.

After that sad task was completed, the white Honda van

where thirteen-year-old Beau lost his life was sealed and towed by a private company provided through USAA, the carriers of the policy on the vehicle, to the Tampa Police Department impound lot to be processed for evidence.

The search of the home where the crime occurred had been thorough and was now complete. Law enforcement removed a vast array of pharmaceutical evidence from the home, including seventeen clonazepam, ninety-one lithium in two separate containers, seventy-five benzatropine, twenty amoxicillin, four triazolam, eight venlafaxin hydrochloride, fifty warfarin, forty-one buspirone, sixty-eight lamotrigine, fifty-nine coumadin, twenty-nine citalopram, a white pharmacy bag with seven loose pills of unknown identity, and two bottles for oxycodone, one with a water bottle cap inside.

They also collected a pile of paperwork; $689 mostly in $20 bills; a purple koozie or foam can cover; nineteen cigarette butts, three cigarettes, a blue lighter, and an empty pack; three cell phones; two purses; jewelry; family photos; five computers; and, of course, everything connected to the gun purchased by Julie Schenecker from the receipt and manual to the live ammunition and spent cartridges and the weapon's original box.

Detective Prebich made one final walk through the fateful home, securing and locking windows and doors. He then stepped out of the house and carried the keys back to headquarters.

As darkness fell, on the evening of the discovered tragedy at the Schenecker home, they came one by one to Hampton Park—friends of Calyx and Beau, neighbors of the family, teachers, and others impacted by the horrific, inexplicable crime so close to home. Soon, nearly two hundred people, many dressed in black, had gathered to honor the memory of this sister and brother whose lives were lost in two coldly calculated moments of violence.

They pulled out lighters and lit their candles with reverence, passing the flame to anyone who needed one. To the sound of shuffling feet, sobs, and sniffles they marched to-gether to the gate of the Ashleigh Reserve of the Tampa Palms subdivision where Beau and Calyx once lived.

Tears streamed down inconsolable faces. Spontaneous hugs flashed like an infection through the crowd. Calyx's seventh-grade teacher stepped to the front of the mourning crowd and said, "You all should remember that you made her life happy."

Those who knew Calyx believed that if she could look down and see them now, she would be happy to see so many friends gathered there, but, at the same time, she'd be a bit embarrassed knowing that she was the reason for all the fuss. Beau's friends were there to remember him but, being younger, remained silent as the older teenagers spoke. Everyone—both children and adults—struggled to make sense of a crime that really made no sense at all.

Dr. Kirsh stood before them and said, "Anyone who wants or needs—parents or kids, it doesn't matter, anyone—can come to the community club tomorrow to talk."

As they walked away, they placed candles around the edge of the oval garden plot at the entrance. Thus ended a horrific day of lost innocence and shattered security for the young friends of Beau and Calyx Schenecker.

Jacob Gassen came home from the event depleted from sorrow, sadness, and shock at the events that unfolded that day. To help him cope, he wrote a poem to Calyx, "Strange Little Running Girl." He recalled the sweetness, simplicity, and kindness of her personality, the strangeness, innocence, and purity of her soul, her quirky, odd, and unique collection of friends, and the shot that ended her life. He wrote about the embarrassment Calyx would feel at their collective worry and ended with encouraging words that she should keep running toward her goals.

To some extent, life still moved on. That night, the sched-uled Class 5A, District 9, tournament was scheduled at King High School's Bill Stewart Stadium. Those who competed that night did so under a flag flying at half-mast.

* * *

Meanwhile, Julie's life in institutionalized captivity had begun. First she was transported to the Orient Road Jail for processing. After fingerprinting, photo taking, and paperwork completion, she was moved to her new home as one of the thirty-three hundred inmates of the Falkenburg Road Jail. She was expected to remain there at least until her bond hearing.

Julie's shaking grew so intense, however, that she was taken to Tampa General Hospital just before midnight. She was scheduled to appear in court the first thing Saturday morning, but that hearing was delayed while she was being treated by doctors in a guarded room.

Saturday morning, Dr. Kirsh knocked on a neighbor's door and asked if she could take care of her children while she was talking to people up at the club. The neighbor readily agreed—the increased closeness and unity with one another in that community was amazing and very healing.

So many people showed up at the club that Dr. Kirsh recruited two colleagues to volunteer their services with her that day. They talked to the children in age-appropriate groups. Many of the high school students brought up the story of another teenager, who went to King and then to Freedom High School. A month earlier, he'd gotten into a fight with his parents and ridden off on his bike. The next morning, he was found dead. None of them knew why he died; they just knew he was gone. The murders resurrected the pain and fear of that last loss, intensifying the students' anxiety. Every loss caused a reactivation of the one the preceded it.

The middle school kids remembered a much-loved art teacher at the nearby elementary school who'd taught them all in earlier years. He was riding his bicycle to school one November day when he was hit by a car driven by another teacher and died. The children had not yet gotten over his death and now another piled on top. The students in that age group were the most traumatized. At that critical age when they are questioning their own identity, trying to find their place in the world, and testing the limits with rebellion, they are most vulnerable to lasting effects from trauma.

All of the teenagers had lost their natural sense of immortality. All of the pupils had to cope with the fact that they had parents, too, and their whole concept of parents had just been challenged. They needed to talk about it to find a way to accept these changes without undue fear.

The elementary school pupils were thinking of the art teacher, too. The pupils also possessed the darkest fears of the parents. They wanted to talk about the worries that one of their parents would snap and kill them, too.

All of the kids shared their memories of Calyx, Beau, or both of them. What shocked them all the most was who committed the crime. They knew Julie. They liked her. They all thought she was a nice, kind person. It made no sense to them at all.

The adults who visited the club that day were in a state of shock and disbelief. The sense of safety had evaporated. Their worldview was shattered. "Everyone felt guilty," Dr. Kirsh said. "There were multiple red flags that we just didn't see."

She talked a lot to parents who wanted to protect their children. Most of them wanted to tell their kids: "She was out of her mind. This is not something that normally happens in life. Let's move on." Dr. Kirsh explained the importance of allowing their children to talk as much and as long about the deaths as they needed to help them process and heal.

The three psychologists remained at the club until seven that evening. Some of the teenagers, who'd been there all day, still didn't want to leave.

After the end of the day, Dr. Kirsh worried about her neighbors. Raised in Israel, she had experienced an entirely different way that people grieved from what she found in this country. After a funeral in Israel, mourning consumes every aspect of life for seven days. Family members sit on low stools or on the floor. They wear torn clothing; do not shave; cut their hair, wear cosmetics, or bathe; and cover the mirrors in their homes. In short, they do nothing but mourn. During the next month, mourners do not attend weddings or any events with music—they don't even listen to music—and continue not to shave or cut their hair. It is a total-immersion approach that is designed to drain away the worst of the grief and prepare the mourner to go on with life.

In this country, people encourage one another to celebrate the life of those who passed even at funerals and memorial services. Grievers are asked to be joyful for having known the deceased rather than wallowing in the selfishness of missing them now that they're gone. To Dr. Kirsh, Americans seemed always determined to be strong, move on, and overcome. Whether it was grief, emotional problems, or mental illness, this culture expected everyone to pull themselves together with willpower and determination.

Ann Sloane, one of the shattered teenagers at the vigil, had started a new page on Facebook, "R.I.P. Beau & Calyx Schenecker," on Friday to honor "two amazing people." By the end of Saturday, the site had drawn more than fifty-five hundred fans.

The participants were located all over the country and across the globe. Some knew the children, but many more were drawn there by the horror of the story. Beau's friends left wistful comments in his memory:

"Beau was a good boy. He'll be dearly missed."

"You were the best friend I ever had. That will never change."

"Beau, we love you. You were the best guy I ever met in 5th grade."

Calyx's friends also dropped by to express their grief:

"Calyx Schenecker was the sweetest girl. I ran track with her for two years . . . to see her picture just makes me cry . . . she will be loved and missed and always remembered for the goodness she had in her heart."

"Dedicating my track season to you, Calyx."

"You'll be missed in art history): . . . Nothing will be the same without your creative sketchbooks!"

Others wrote about both of the teenagers:

"I knew Beau and Calyx from Germany. I grew up with both of them and I hope they know they did not deserve . . ." to have this happen.

"I know my mum won't kill me. She would never."

Many negative comments about Julie Schenecker and a desire for the death penalty popped up on the page. Ann reminded people that the page was for Calyx and Beau and not about their mother, what she did, or how she should be punished. Her pleas fell on many deaf ears.

Then it grew much worse with the arrival of the forces of negativity known as trolls in internet slang—individuals who had no connection to the deceased but simply roamed the Internet looking for opportunities to exploit the pain of others, mocking the grief of the mourning participants in the group. They ridiculed Calyx and Beau—some making obscene comments. They voiced approval of Julie's actions. These angry, bitter people who felt threatened by the presence of harmony anywhere created such a surge of distress that Ann had to shut down comments until she could get assistance to moderate the site.

Over the next few days, many more Facebook memorials popped up—all filled with heartfelt messages and all plagued with the same problems arising from the dark side of the Web.

Beyond those pages, the Internet filled with people wanting to reach out and comfort. On Parker's Facebook page, a graduate of Fort Worth Country Day School wrote: "Please pray for the entire Schenecker family!!! ALL need our prayers for peace, strength AND forgiveness!! We MUST pray!!! CDS alums, how can we ever forget the support of Eddie Schenecker for ALL those years, our support for the family can NEVER stop. God will NEVER leave Parker's side and neither can we!!"

On a blog for runners, Coach Gary Bingham left a message expressing gratitude for prayers extended to him during this trying time and asked for prayers for Parker Schenecker as well as for the track team. "We may be small in numbers but every one of them have big hearts and are great friends to each other."

On Saturday evening, youth pastor Sarah Fuller opened the doors of St. James United Methodist Church in Tampa Palms to forty teenagers, Calyx's former classmates at Benito Middle as well as friends from high school and a dozen Liberty Middle students who knew Beau. For an hour, the students poured out their grief with tears spilling down their cheeks. When it was over, they left the room cluttered with near-empty tissue boxes and wastebaskets piled high with crumpled white tissues. It was the first time many of them had ever experienced the death of anyone in their lives.

Sunday morning, Julie was released from the hospital and transported back to the Falkenburg Road Jail, which housed the largest infirmary on Florida's west coast. She was placed in a medical confinement cell, all alone, at her request.

She had no access to television or newspapers. She could leave her cell for one hour each day during recreation time to take a shower, use the phone, or go outdoors. Her actions that past Thursday took her from being a mother with an envied, loving family to being just another prisoner, swallowed up in the heartless reality of institutional life.

CHAPTER 31

Up in Iowa that Sunday morning, Julie's former volleyball teammate Lisa Pilch rose from bed with an untroubled mind. She had yet to hear the horrific news tumbling out of Florida.

She sat down to watch *Good Morning America* as she got ready for the day. When the shocking story about the Schenecker tragedy came flying out of the news announcer's lips, Lisa nearly fell on the floor. At first, she couldn't believe it. When acceptance seeped into her thoughts, she knew that Julie could not have been in her right mind when she committed that unspeakable act.

Crying, Lisa signed on to the Internet to try to learn more. The whole time she searched and read, an unrelenting mantra pounded in her head: *I can't believe this. I can't believe this.*

Sunday morning, Detective Gary Sandel started his day at the medical examiner's office, where the autopsies of Calyx and Beau Schenecker were scheduled that day. There Sandel met with Detective Danny Rhodes and Crime Scene Technician Matthew Evans. After the procedure began, Sandel turned over the observation responsibilities to Rhodes and Evans and went out to MacDill Air Force Base for his first meeting with the victims' next of kin, Colonel Parker Schenecker.

Rhodes and Evans would rather not be standing by these stainless-steel tables. Their presence at autopsies was necessary but not something they ever approached with any shred of enjoyment. This situation was worse than most, though, because the bodies belonged to two children who should have lived decades longer.

Dr. Adams and his assistant removed and reinventoried the clothing of Calyx Schenecker, noting that the items were "unremarkable except for some blood staining." The medical examiner then made a meticulous search of the exterior of the body, describing everything he observed down to the gold-colored polish on her toenails.

He noted just one scar on the front of her right shoulder, no tattoos, and no recent injuries prior to the traumatic event that took her life. He then recorded the graphic detail regarding the bullet wound inflicted to the back of her head and face, including the location, size, shape, and path. He indicated that there was no stippling, soot, or muzzle stamp demonstrating that it was not a contact wound.

There were no exit wounds. He recovered two copper-jacketed projectiles—both consisting of two separate pieces, the jacket itself and the lead slug. Then, even though the cause of death seemed obvious, he continued the procedure, with a thorough analysis of all her internal organs. He found nothing out of the ordinary for a young adolescent female. The toxicology report ultimately reported no suspicious or illegal substances in her body.

Next, Adams began the autopsy on Beau. The results were quite similar—only the age, sex, and position of the projectiles changed and, in this case, there was an exit wound.

The conclusions for both of the children were the same: cause of death "gunshot wound of the head with perforation of the skull and brain"; and manner of death "homicide—shot by other person(s) with handgun(s)."

Detective Sandel's task, though not as viscerally unpleasant, was still an onerous one—speaking to a family member of the deceased. At least the death notification was out of the way and he would not have to be the first to deliver that unwelcome news.

Parker's friend Colonel Hamby met Sandel at the front gate of MacDill and escorted him back to his on-base residence. The distraught father waited for Sandel there. Parker hid his grief behind a steely, stoic front in keeping with his military background and rank. "My wife has battled depression for more than ten years and had checked herself into rehab centers several times in the past for substance abuse and alcohol," he said. He paused, closed his eyes, and shook his head before he continued. "I knew she had depression issues, but I never thought she would do something like this to our kids."

"Could you provide the names of the rehab facilities where she stayed?" the detective asked.

"Yes"—he nodded—"when time permits. Right now, my focus is to have the kids taken to Texas for a funeral, after the autopsies are done."

The tragedy of the crime swept over Sandel. Two dead children, one parent consumed by grief, and another locked behind bars: Could family dysfunction get any worse?

CHAPTER 32

The pilgrimage to the Scheneckers' community of Ashleigh Reserve continued unabated throughout the weekend, with visitors dropping off tributes on the pile before they left. By Monday morning, a blanket of flowers, candles, teddy bears, handwritten notes and cards to Beau and Calyx, and copies of *Fantastic Beasts and Where to Find Them* and *Harry Potter and the Goblet of Fire* piled up on the ground outside of the gate—a visual reminder to everyone who lived there as they departed for work, school, and appointments at the beginning of a new week.

Some of the parents were glad to see that outpouring of remembrance and grief, thinking it was a positive, healing component that would help them all get past the trauma. Others wanted it all to go away—the tributes cleared—nothing physically there to remind their children of what had happened so close to home. These parents also resented the presence of the media—the phone calls, the vehicles, the pervasive nature of the stories in print, on the radio, and on their televisions.

At 9:00 a.m., the Homicide Squad of the Tampa Police Department met to review leads and assign the next steps in the investigation. Detective Sandel and Crime Scene Technician

Evans went to the impound lot to process the vehicle removed from the Royal Park Court garage.

Searching the interior, Sandel found a projectile under the passenger's side rear seat. Evans photographed it where it was found and took custody of the bullet. They also retrieved and bagged as evidence Beau's eyeglasses that had been left on the dashboard, another pair of eyeglasses found in the vehicle, and a dry-cleaning receipt.

At Liberty Middle School and King High School, the school administration released the crisis intervention teams to help both students and teachers cope with their overwhelming emotions and deal with their unexpected loss. As everyone arrived at the schools that day, all took note of the flag, fluttering at half-mast.

At C. Leon King High, Principal Bruning's voice rang out through the speakers in each classroom, asking for a moment of silence: "I need to make an announcement about the tragic loss of Calyx Schenecker at the end of last week." She went on to explain the availability of counseling services. But she mentioned no details of how Calyx lost her life.

At King, the counselors watched the students moving through the hallways, far more subdued than usual. The school was filled with quiet murmurs and muffled footsteps as if they feared waking the dead. Here and there, in the clumps of students, some wore Harry Potter gear in honor of their fallen classmate.

The counselors warned students not to internalize the tragedy and draw conclusions from it and apply the experience to their own lives. Many of them were wondering about their personal safety. They knew they'd talked back to their parents. They couldn't help worrying that the same thing could happen to them.

When one would voice that fear aloud, a counselor would ask if they'd had any fights with their parents in the last week. Students would admit they had—many saying it happened a lot of times, maybe every day. Then they would be asked about the end result. Almost universally, the kids said they were grounded. Being able to confront their fear and voice the reality of their punishment put many minds at ease.

At Liberty Middle School, Vito Ricciardi, a school psychologist, led the counseling team. He met first with the school administration to discuss the violent nature of the crime, the "why" question, and the need to return the school, teachers, and students to a state of homeostasis and balance.

His team commandeered the library to get his team ready for the first influx of students. Before the instructional day began, he met with the faculty, both to help them normalize and acknowledge their own grief and to help them cope with the children facing one of the most stressful times in their lives.

"This is going to be a challenging day for you—your kids are torn up. You're probably grieving Beau. Put your grief on a shelf and focus on the kids for four or five hours.

"You never know which kid lost a grandma last month, which student has parents divorcing, which lost a dog the week before. Even if they don't know why they want to go to the library, allow them to come."

He spoke briefly about dealing with the range of reactions from the students and told the faculty to expect everything from children who internalized all their pain and withdrew to those who were displaying anger and aggression, lashing out at everyone around them. He reminded the teachers that in extreme cases action needed to be taken immediately, because for kids reacting to pain "the only difference between suicide and homicide is the direction they pointed the gun."

"Remember, a smile, a hand on the shoulder, will let them know that you—that all adults—are there to take care of them."

The bell rang and the school day started with a moment of silence. Then the invitation to come to the library went out to all students in need of grief counseling.

Twenty different therapists sat down with groups of six

kids at a time. As the students settled into their chairs, the counselors said, "I didn't know Beau. Tell me about him."

Using Beau's class schedule as a guide, Vito went from one classroom to another speaking to larger groups of children. Most of them wanted someone to explain to them how a mother could kill her children. It was a question without any satisfactory answer.

In every one of these classrooms, he saw a disproportionate number of kids wearing blue. He suspected that there was a reason and he was right: Blue was Beau's favorite color.

Ricciardi tried to help the students understand their own feelings by comparing their intense emotional pain to the physical pain of an injury. He acknowledged the students' grief and drew a parallel between the emotional agony they felt now and the physical pain they felt the last time they were cut or broke a bone. "You have to open the wound, to look at and examine it," he said. "Then you have to cleanse the wound to keep infection away," he continued, pointing to similar catharsis from emotional pain they received when they talked about it with others.

He asked them, "When you first heard the news, what did you think?" He listened as they spoke up—some for the first time.

Vito then planted seeds to grow their coping mechanisms by talking about closing up the wound. "Sometimes we lose someone we care about and it makes us think about those losses. Did anyone here lose anyone before?" As hands went up, he asked each one, "How did you cope?"

The students shared their experiences, giving strength to one another. Then, Vito talked to them about aftercare for their wound: "You might not sleep well for a while. You might have stomachaches and headaches. You might not like your favorite video game. But be assured, every hour that goes by, you are healing a little more." He reminded them that ignoring wounds can lead to infection and told them they needed to deal with the emotional injuries in just the same way.

Unlike the high school students, Vito did not find any of the younger students at the middle school who expressed any concerns about their personal safety. Since all of these children were from upper-middle-class backgrounds and none had known deprivation or experienced drug abuse by their parents or engaged in that behavior themselves, they felt firmly secure in their innocence.

Children that age don't really understand the permanence of death, Vito explained, yet they were very angry at the injustice of parental betrayal and furious with the "crazy lady." Vito repeatedly heard the refrain, "This is not supposed to happen here."

"Every one of the students was frustrated because no one could give them the answer to the existential question of 'why?'" Vito said, and admitted that he couldn't do it, either, but he explained, "You cannot apply a logical explanation to someone who is delusional or a borderline psychotic. None of our logic works."

Throughout the day, students paraded outside to leave tributes—flowers, candles, and cards—to their classmate Beau. On the exterior wall, above these remembrances, someone hung Beau's soccer jersey, which was filled with signatures by day's end.

Exhausted by the draining tasks of absorbing the intense emotional turmoil of the children, most of the counselors were ready to leave right after the students to marshal their resources for the next day. But they were still needed and remained on campus to meet with the members of the faculty in need of their help and advice.

Vito could see the pain and emotional exhaustion in each face as the teacher entered the library. He tried to patch them up as best as he could, preparing them to face the next day.

The team returned and counseled children on Tuesday and remained available all week in the faculty lounge to deal with any problems they had with students and any issues they were having with their own personal grief.

Vito was impressed with the bravery and dedication of

the teachers. During the day, they tabled their own grief and helped the kids to bounce back. The natural resilience of the children would set in with time. The school would recover its equilibrium, but he knew no one there would ever forget.

CHAPTER 33

Before her first appearance before a judge on Monday afternoon, Julie filed an affidavit requesting the services of the public defender's office. On it, she listed her assets, including $20,000 in a bank account, $120,000 in mutual funds, $2,850 in rental income, $14,000 in savings, and 17,000 dollars' worth of equity in real estate. She put an asterisk next to them, noting: "Owned with husband."

In the motion filed in support of her claim, Assistant Public Defender Robert Frasier wrote: "In the event Defendant's husband proceeds to dissolve their marriage, two cars owned by the Defendant and the money market account will be marital assets subject to equitable distribution. Julie listed more than $800,000 in liabilities and debts. She listed her number of dependents as zero."

That Monday afternoon, Julie did not appear in the courtroom, but she was present via closed-circuit television from the jail for the announcement of the foregone conclusion concerning the possibility of bail. In the courtroom were her two representatives from the public defender's office, Robert Frasier, a veteran criminal defense attorney who had defended thirty-four first-degree murder cases, almost half involving the death penalty. Maura Doherty stood by his side to assist.

Julie was called to the podium. She did not speak; she

stood before the camera, weeping, shaking, and clutching a tissue. Her tears continued throughout the two-minute appearance.

Judge Walter Heinrich addressed her: "Due to the nature of your charges and the strength of the case against you at this point, miss, you are obviously going to be held in jail without bond. I assume in the future, the defense will request the appointment of doctors. That's something that'll be taking place after they file the appropriate motions. You are excused."

Another start-up Facebook page, The Official Calyx & Beau Schenecker Memorial Page, had garnered over two thousand fans by the end of Monday—just three days after their deaths were known. It called on the students at King High to wear green, black, and silver on Tuesday—another reference to the Harry Potter books. "After a successful first day in remembrance of Calyx with an amazing turn-out of Harry Potter gear—we want to keep it up and do Slytherin colors tomorrow!☺"

Slytherin was the name of one of the four houses at the Hogwarts School of Witchcraft and Wizardry. It was the traditional home for students who were cunning, resourceful, and ambitious.

In response to the unending requests for information about Colonel Parker Schenecker, CENTCOM at MacDill Air Force Base released a statement on Tuesday, February 1: "Colonel Parker Schenecker has returned from his deployment and is grieving with family and friends. He is devoted first and foremost to honoring the lives and memory of his beautiful children, Calyx and Beau. Parker and his family have been touched by the overwhelming support from the community both near and abroad. Arrangements and details are still being finalized with regard to the services to be held for Calyx and Beau."

CHAPTER 34

That Tuesday, Detective Sandel went to Beau's school, Liberty Middle in Tampa Palms, to meet with the young man's teachers. School staff placed Sandel in a conference room near the main office. Each of Beau's instructors reported there for a short interview.

History teacher David Calhoun said, "Beau's a good student. We joked together about sports and video games." He added, "Beau never mentioned any issues at home and appeared to be a very happy kid." In response to the detective's question about his student's attendance, he said that he thought Beau had been absent on Wednesday but could not be certain without checking his records.

Sophie Dikizeko, Beau's French teacher, said, "He was an A student in my class and was rarely absent. He was an active participant in class and asked questions regularly." She, too, did not recall Beau mentioning any problems at home.

Beau's tech teacher, Daisy Questella, had been his business instructor for the past two years: "He's one of my best students. He was a happy and respectful kid." A sad smile crossed her face, and she added, "He was so excited about making the school soccer team." She thought Beau might have been absent from school on Monday but was not certain. He never talked to her about his home situation, either.

Language arts teacher Allison Newton said, "Beau had been a C student, but he recently dropped to a 'D.' I sent a note home to advise his parents of the grades, but I never heard back from them." She believed that Beau had been absent on Monday and Wednesday of the last week.

"Did he ever mention any issues at home?"

Ms. Newton furrowed her brow. "No, he hadn't," she said.

The science teacher Stephanie Jones was the next to enter the conference room: "Beau is a well-liked student with a great attitude. I've known him since sixth grade." She knew that he missed school on Monday because he told her that he'd slept in late and his mother didn't want to bring him to school.

Beau's physical education teacher, Jessica Rosquette, had also known Beau since sixth grade: "He's a very competitive kid. He never mentioned any problems in his home environment."

Math teacher Melissa Grier echoed the comments of many others about his home life and said that Beau was a typical B-C eighth grader.

Across town, Detective Sonja Wise mirrored Sandel, going to the C. Leon King High School, walking through halls filled with students decked in silver, green, and black. She talked to the teachers who taught Calyx. Her track/cross-country coach, Gary Bingham, had a bit more insight into the Schenecker family than any of the Liberty teachers seemed to have.

He said that Calyx had been a member of the track team for two years: "I've met and spoken to the entire family during that time, both at track meets and at sport banquets."

"Did you observe any problems between Calyx and her mother?"

"Not that I've seen," he answered. "But back in October, Mr. Schenecker told me that Calyx may not be attending all the practices and meets because she was being disrespectful to her mother. He also said that the whole family was in counseling."

"When did you last see Calyx?" Wise asked.

"Thursday, January twenty-seventh, at track practice, from three to four thirty. Calyx said her mom was there to pick her up and she left."

"Did you see her mother?"

"No," Mr. Bingham said. "I saw the white van but did not see Mrs. Schenecker."

"What was your impression of Mrs. Schenecker?"

"She appeared to be fine at times and, at other times, she seemed kinda not all together or zoned out."

"And Calyx?"

"She was always happy and smiling."

IB trigonometry teacher Shauna Shaw said that this year was the first time she ever taught Calyx and she knew nothing personal about her: "She was very respectful, had a good attitude, and appeared to be very sociable with her friends." Shaw added that Calyx had, however, requested a recommendation for a boarding school in Miami.

Paul Jannereth, AP European history instructor, agreed with Mrs. Shaw's impressions regarding Calyx's interactions with her peers. "She had an 'A' in my class."

"Calyx was a good student—very focused on her studies. I had no reason for concern about her well-being," IB English teacher Twila Dickerson said.

AP art history teacher Michele Prado said, "Calyx was quite bright and very focused, but she always seemed tired."

Her AP human geography instructor, Karly Dell, remembered Calyx as a refreshingly innocent and friendly student: "I didn't observe anything that would cause alarm."

Chemistry teacher Vithal Patel said that Calyx never interacted with him but noted that she was very bright. Carly Eslick, her Spanish teacher, was the only one who said Calyx struggled in class. And homeroom teacher Lindsey Plyer said, "Calyx is focused and polite, but my contact with her was very limited."

Rusty Davidson said that Calyx had been in his physics class for just three weeks and he never had any interaction with her.

IB counselor Rosanna Hoit told Detective Wise that she was familiar with Calyx and her family: "In ninth grade, I counseled her about academic concerns. She was able to overcome her perceived obstacles and excelled in her classes."

"Were you aware of any problems in her home?" Wise asked.

"I knew about the case with the Department of Children and Families. They called me in October or November last year. I returned their call and told them there was no record of issues with Calyx based on her physical appearance, academic standing, or behavior."

"When did you last see Calyx?"

"I talked to her on Thursday about her request for a recommendation to boarding school. I asked her to bring me a list of her extracurricular activities and interests so that I could include them in my letter. Calyx promised to bring that in on Friday." But by Friday, Calyx was already dead.

Not one of the teachers observed any evidence of or heard Calyx speak about any problems at home. None of them ever conducted any parental meetings or conferences.

In the context of logic, one would expect that it would take an escalating, rampant course of misbehavior to push a parent into violence against their teenage children. But, in this case, the opposite was true. Two very good, well-behaved children were killed through no fault of their own.

CHAPTER 35

Tragedies, although they can bring out the best in people, also have a tendency to stir the despicable into action. Bogus memorial fund-raising happened after horrific damage caused by Hurricane Katrina and in the aftermath of the devastating earthquake in Haiti. The murders of the Schenecker children brought out the mercenary parasites to feed on the sorrow and horror of this crime, as well.

One phony fund draped in military mufti claimed to be raising money for Beau's soccer team and Calyx's cross-country squad. People typing in "Julie Schenecker" on Google or other search engines found links directing them to You-Tube videos about celebrities, partially clothed women, and an apparent pyramid scheme.

Parker issued a warning on the morning of February 2. He said that the family had not yet set up anything: "Any such website which bears the Schenecker name is unauthorized, misleading, and merely an attempt to exploit this tragedy and deepen the sorrow of a community trying to heal."

Another piece of darkness fell on the day when the West-boro Baptist Church announced their plans for a protest beginning at 5:15 p.m. and lasting until the beginning of that night's memorial service for the Schenecker children. The congregation has made a habit of trumpeting their convictions while disrupting funeral services connected to the military and to the deaths of homosexuals.

The revolting statement released by Pastor Fred Phelps and director of creative ministries Josh Saliba read: "God sent the shooter to Tampa, Florida. . . . Murderous mother kills rebellious children while father is off playing bloody war games, fighting for same sex marriage. GOD SMACK! . . . The mother is a military wife and the doomed American military declared war on God & His church."

A group opposing the church's mission, the Florida West Coast Riders, promised to be on hand with American flags unfurled to help shield family and friends from the potentially hurtful messages on the signs carried by the disturbed and disturbing protestors. "It doesn't matter to them at all. They get out there with their bull horns and their nasty signs and they get attention . . . that's what they want," said Thomas Brown of the Florida West Coast Riders. "They're all about being offensive and we do what we do in a respectful way."

Despite their threats to the contrary, the Westboro flock did not show up. Their statement was sufficient to meet their desires: creating fear and anxiety in the mourners and garnering attention for them, their church, and their warped viewpoint.

At six o'clock that evening, King High and Liberty Middle Schools sponsored a celebration of life service at First Baptist Church in Temple Terrace. The memorial event was closed to the general public; only students and teachers at the two schools were allowed to attend.

Hundreds packed the sanctuary. Parker Schenecker sat in the front room listening as friends and teachers stepped up to share memories of the Schenecker children. The grieving father stood to hug each person after they finished speaking.

A video played with a series of photos of Calyx and Beau. In the background, Lee Ann Womack sang "I Hope You Dance." Throughout the showing, Parker wiped away tears—as did many around him.

Teenagers played instruments. The gathered mourners

sang "Amazing Grace." Parker was the last person to stand behind the podium. Speaking publicly for the first time since the tragedy devastated his life, he said, "I can't thank you enough for today's moving, loving memorial for my exceptional children, and for your tributes through the past few days. Whether you wore some blue or some Harry Potter glasses," he said with a bittersweet smile stealing across his face, "whether you lit a candle, laid a flower, or signed a soccer jersey, you honored my children, your devoted friend, your classmate, your teammate.

"The family and I are humbled by your support, grace, and overwhelming love for Calyx and Beau. They love you, too. Please don't forget how they lived."

Not one person mentioned Julie Schenecker. Not a word was spoken about how the two teenagers died.

Pastor J. P. Clouse prayed at the end of service referring to all the things nobody said: "There's a lot of people out here that have real feelings of hurt, questions of why. It's hard. And that's okay."

In the lobby, after the ninety-minute service, a long line formed to write messages to the kids whose photos were perched on a table—Calyx wearing a red clown nose, running cross-country, dancing, and acting goofy with her friends; Beau always smiling, sometimes looking mischievous.

Language arts teacher Allison Newton swore that in her classroom Beau's seat would remain empty for the rest of the year in memory of the young boy whom no one would ever forget.

On February 3, Patty Powers got to see her daughter for the first time since her arrest. With a few other family members, Patty visited with Julie for almost an hour.

Parker signed a release, on February 4, signing over the white Honda van to the USAA insurance company. Doubtless, he never wanted to see that vehicle again.

The following day, Parker attended a memorial service at MacDill Air Force Base. The one-hour private service at the base included speakers, music, and a video tribute to Calyx and Beau. The predominately military audience, who, for the most part did not know the children, attended to honor the grief of the father and fellow serviceman.

Parker stood before them and said, "Today is another day on our journey to healing. While sadness seems to lurk right behind us every step of the way, I assure you that today's wonderful tribute to my children will keep me looking ahead."

Parker had one more memorial ordeal to endure, the most final one of all, the funeral of his children in his hometown of Fort Worth. In advance of the service, lengthy obituaries ran in the *Fort Worth Star-Telegram*. It included the times for the memorial service and details of family left behind along with praise for the lives the children led and the essence of who they were.

On the morning of Tuesday, February 8, Calyx and Beau were laid to rest in a private burial ceremony, conducted by Wittich Funeral Home. At 2:30 that afternoon, more than one hundred mourners entered the fifteen-hundred-seat auditorium at the nondenominational Christ Chapel Bible Church, in the Arlington Heights neighborhood, for the memorial service.

It was a more formal setting than the previous remembrances, complete with flickering candles and a grand piano on the stage to accompany soloists and the congregation as they joined together to sing hymns. A white cross adorned with a large arrangement of white roses stood in front of the speakers' podium.

Only two people addressed this audience, Senior Pastor Ted Kitchens and Parker Schenecker, but the same video was shown as at earlier memorials featuring photographs of baby Beau on the beach and in action shots from his soccer games and Calyx dressed as a fairy and competing at track meets.

Pastor Kitchens spoke of the relatives and friends whose lives had been brushed by the unique spirits of Calyx and Beau: "This afternoon, we celebrate their lives, in Jesus' name."

He said that though it was impossible to understand how God could allow a tragic end to such brief lives, everything—good and bad—is part of a grand plan. Pastor Kitchens assured them all that Calyx and Beau were not hurting: "They are looking over their shoulders and they see us coming.

"Someday God will reveal the reason to us and that's our hope." He remembered Calyx and Beau as leaders in their own young ways. Calyx, he said, had recently helped organize a fund-raiser relay for the American Cancer Society that netted more than one hundred thousand dollars. He said that one of her relatives called her sublime and said she was a mature soul inside a young body, filled with life and light. Beau was known for his energy and sensitivity to others: "What could have been is remarkable."

Then, the grieving father stepped up on the stage and shredded the emotions of everyone in the room. He began, "First and foremost, my family would like to thank Christ Chapel Bible Church, Dr. Ted Kitchens, and Bill Runyon for opening your doors and hearts to us. Mom, Edmund, this homecoming was absolutely the right decision."

Parker paused before beginning the body of his address. He looked down, then raised his head to look at the crowd: "Silence, brothers, innocent spirits have passed by." His eyes looked heavenward as he paused again. "As I mourn the loss of my loved dear children, I am comforted that they have both been welcomed to the other side, and heaven is rejoicing in their coming.

"I will deeply miss Calyx and Beau. And I have a feeling that even though some of you didn't know them well or at all, through Dr. Kitchens' kind words and this beautiful service, you now feel their presence—something the rest of us know all too well. Today, we celebrate the way they lived, and I will spend the rest of my life doing just that.

"I encourage others, especially those who join me in mourning Calyx and Beau, to help keep the essence of their spirits alive by being kind to others and by living their lives with purpose. I know my children were loved; they knew they were loved; now we all must go forward to honor them with love and respect for each other.

"Hug your children—every chance you get. Draw your loved ones closer to you so that you may love and be loved. And, if I may be so bold, if this grieving dad can ask you just one thing: Remember Calyx and Beau Schenecker and rejoice for having known them."

After the service, he released a statement about his loss to the media that ended with this exhortation: "Help keep the essence of their spirits alive by being kind to others, by working and playing hard, and by living your lives with purpose."

CHAPTER 36

On February 10, the grand jury met to consider Julie Schenecker's case. At the end of their deliberations, they released an indictment charging her with two counts of murder in the first degree, premeditated. Count one alleged that she

did unlawfully and feloniously kill a human being, to wit: Beau Schenecker, with a premeditated design to effect the death of Beau Schenecker or any other human being by shooting him with a weapon, to wit: a firearm, and during the course of the commission of the offense, the said Julie Schenecker carried, displayed, used or threatened to use, or attempted to use a weapon, to wit: a firearm, and actually possessed a firearm and discharged a firearm, and as a result of the discharge, death was inflicted upon Beau Schenecker, contrary to the form of the statute in such cases made and provided.

The language in the second count was identical to the first. The only difference was that in the place of Julie's son's name "Calyx Schenecker" was entered into the official legal language of the charge. Julie was now eligible for the death penalty. The only decision that remained for the state was whether or not they would pursue it. The stage was set for her next appearance in court.

* * *

The next day at the C. Leon King High School, students gathered in the interior courtyard to make one of Calyx's dreams come true. They planted the willow Calyx wanted to see on the campus, representing the Whomping Willow in the Harry Potter books. Around it were commemorative bricks: one engraved with Calyx's name embraced by hearts and the message "No Ostuary Left Behind"; another with the words "Battle On" flanked by lightning, below that "Dumbledore's Army"; and the one from good friend Tatiana Henry read: "Our friendship is immortal. Miss you."

Latanya Henry brought bundles of yellow and red daisies and passed them out to the teenagers. The three Ostuaries, Sara, Jena, and Tatiana, were the first to drop the flowers at the base of the tree.

They addressed the crowd, saying that the final tribute to Calyx would come in the decades ahead. They promised that as they left high school, went to college, and grew into women they would never forget the girl who wanted to go to three colleges at once, live in New York, and see the elephants of Thailand. Sara Wortman summed it all up when she said, "I hope I do something with my life, because Calyx wanted to do everything."

By the time the dedication was over, the ground and decorative bricks around the tree were covered with a blanket of yellow and red flowers, dropped there one by one. One last remembrance remained. Sara tied a ribbon around the trunk of the tree. And typically of the interaction among these teenage friends, Tatiana said, "The bow isn't perky enough."

At 8:30 in the morning on February 16, Julie Schenecker appeared before Judge Ashley Moody for the arraignment on charges of murdering her son and daughter. Security was heightened in court that day, because of the concerns generated by the high-profile nature of the case. In addition to the possibility that someone might want to take revenge on Julie, the risk that a person would enter the courtroom in order to attempt to create a scene or make a statement was higher than usual. Everyone, including the media representatives who outnumbered the other spectators, was required to be scanned with magnetic wands before admittance.

With a female deputy on each arm, chains and shackles on her feet, and hands cuffed in front of her, Julie entered the courtroom. She was in better shape than she had been at the time of her arrest. With no signs of shaking and no wild rolling eyes, she looked depressed but calm.

She was dressed in a red two-piece outfit that looked like hospital scrubs except for the big white letters "INMATE" stenciled across her chest. On her feet she wore white socks and cheap tan slip-on sandals. Her hair was stringy, disheveled, and unkempt, with dark roots clearly visible. It cascaded across her face, obscuring the view of one side.

Two lawyers from the public defender's office stood up at the defense table when Judge Moody entered and took her seat. Bob Frasier, gray-haired but with a conspicuous bald spot, wore a black suit and wire-rimmed glasses. Standing beside him, Maura Doherty wore a gray pinstripe suit, with her long brown hair falling a couple of inches past her shoulders.

Frasier addressed the judge: "The record reflects that we were appointed for a first appearance as Ms. Schenecker filed a financial affidavit in accordance with the law that the clerk deemed to disentitle her to services of the public defender.

"We have filed for another determination of that based on the circumstances. The expense of a defense, in this case, is going to be prohibitive and far exceed her family's assets, and, so . . . we respectfully request that the court reappoint the office of the public defender . . . to proceed on Ms. Schenecker's behalf."

The prosecution did not object and the judge allowed the public defender's representation for now. She then moved to the arraignment proceeding itself.

Bob Frasier waived the formal reading of the charges and entered a plea of not guilty on both counts on Julie's behalf. On the defense motion to freeze the marital assets in case they were needed to fund the defense, the judge said she did not have the power to do that and that Parker needed to be party to any such move. She added that she would consider a lien to recover expenses.

Flanked by deputies, Julie sat emotionless in her chair. Her eyes remained closed or downcast throughout it all. She said nothing, reacted to nothing. There was no way for an observer to tell if Julie was even aware of what swirled around her. In less than four minutes, it was over.

After the hearing, the Schenecker family spokesperson released this statement:

> *Colonel Parker Schenecker is currently out of state and was unable to attend Wednesday's arraignment for Julie Schenecker. Currently, he is meeting with family members and close friends to formalize his plans to honor the memory of Calyx and Beau. At the same time, he is considering the best path to help him heal from this tragedy.*
>
> *Parker would like to thank everyone who has reached out to express their love for Calyx and Beau and who have shown support for his family during this difficult time. The generosity and love supporters have shown through letters, phone calls and donations to the Calyx and Beau Memorial Fund has been humbling. Parker has finalized plans for the Fund's first donation: C. Leon King High School's Relay for Life benefitting the American Cancer Society. Calyx's school recently notified Parker that they will honor Calyx by retaining her as Captain of her Harry Potter–inspired "Wizarding Independence Day" team. This contribution is just the first step in keeping his promise to support those causes and activities his children found important.*

CHAPTER 37

On Friday, February 18, 2011, at 7:10 a.m., Parker saw his wife for the first time since he was deployed to the Middle East in mid-January. It was only the second time that Julie had any visitors since her incarceration.

Parker visited Julie in the jail to tell her he wanted a divorce. Although inmates normally talk to relatives via a closed-circuit feed, Colonel Jim Previtera of the Hillsborough County Sheriff's Office made special arrangements. Parker and Julie spoke to each other separated only by Plexiglas.

Julie could have refused his visit, but she didn't. She watched him walk in, sit down, and pick up the receiver. A marital gulf had never been wider.

Parker initiated the conversation, "How about we do this: Let's not talk about anything that happened in the house."

"Yeah, that would be great," she said.

Parker told her about the memorial service held for the children. He explained that they were buried in a Fort Worth cemetery and talked to her about the memorial events both there and here in Tampa. He talked about the children's schools and their friends and the many ways they continued to honor and remember the lives of Calyx and Beau. He and Julie talked for nearly an hour. The meeting was emotional but not volatile.

Toward the end, Parker said, "I want to look you in the eye and tell you that I am going to seek a divorce."

Julie said, "Okay."

After he left, Parker released a public statement:

I felt it was important and proper to inform her in person about my need to focus on the future, and my intention to file for a divorce. Clearly, the events of January 27th have taken Julie and me on different paths. I have said for many days now that I will spend the rest of my life honoring the memory of my two beautiful children, Calyx and Beau. This difficult but necessary step will help me do just that . . . move forward. The meeting was both emotional and productive. We discussed numerous topics but focused mostly on how so many people continue to honor and remember the lives of Calyx and Beau.

Before the day was done papers were filed in court requesting the legal dissolution of their relationship. In his petition, Parker said that his marriage was "irretrievably broken." It continued with: "Wife shot and killed both minor children." In addition to the end of the marriage, it requested a fair distribution of the marital assets and asked that their home be sold.

On the next Monday morning, February 21, Julie agreed to have her assets frozen and a lien imposed to repay the public defenders for representing her in the murder charges. That afternoon at 1:30, Julie was back in court for a hearing about the state's motion to compel saliva samples.

On Wednesday, Parker's divorce attorney Alexander Caballero filed a response to the financial motion filed by the public defenders:

After his children's tragic deaths, Colonel Schenecker could not imagine that there was anything else the defendant could take from him. However, her motion to freeze assets threatens to delay their divorce proceedings. . . . Much more disturbingly, however, it appears to be an attempt to compel Colonel Schenecker—who had only intended to participate in these proceedings to give a voice to his children, the victims—to fund the defense. . . . Aside from being patently unreasonable, the requested relief is not supported in the law.

Caballero further argued that the decision should be made by the divorce courts, not by the judge trying the criminal case. Arguments for and against the motion were scheduled for a hearing the next day before Judge Ashley Moody. The circuit judge ruled that she lacked the authority to grant the motion because Julie had not yet been convicted of a crime.

At King High School, another tribute to Calyx took root. The Biology Club started planting a butterfly garden in her memory that week. They planned to expand it as they had funds available to purchase more plants.

On February 28, the school spoke out again about their classmate. Principal Carla Bruning announced that the sixth annual King High School Relay For Life on March 19–20, 2011, to benefit the American Cancer Society, would be dedicated to sophomore Calyx Schenecker: "What better way to celebrate her life and pay tribute to her loss than through an event that is dedicated to curing a disease that takes the life of so many people?" Bruning added that luminarias would be placed on the track in Calyx's honor and participants would walk a lap right there where she was known to spend hours in practice with the school's track-and-field team.

CHAPTER 38

Before the sixth annual King High School Relay For Life began, the Wizarding Independence Day team had already raised eleven thousand dollars in their quest to meet Calyx's vision of being the relay's top fund-raiser that year. The opening ceremonies kicked off the event at three that afternoon.

Parker arrived and was overwhelmed by the number of people gathered there. He took a moment off by himself to compose his thoughts and emotions. At ten that night, he and more than six hundred people gathered in a football field to honor Calyx and Beau. The lights went dim and the blue and green luminarias, surrounded by photos of Calyx and Beau, lined the football field, creating an otherworldly glow on the faces in front of Parker.

With the King High School PRIDE musical group he stepped up onstage, where the choir sang the words of a song a friend had written in Calyx's honor. It was a collaborative effort, using the words written by Jacob Gassen and music composed by Betsey Giammattei. Parker then addressed the crowd: "Be proud of your accomplishments. I promise you that I am proud of all of you. Calyx and Beau are beaming with devotion and respect for you." He added that the school community understood how to love and to be loved. In a closing question, he asked the crowd if they had ever felt true joy. He presented the American Cancer Society with a check for five thousand dollars, the first contribution made on behalf of the Calyx and Beau Schenecker Memorial Fund.

Parker then invited all to participate in a Harry Potter–themed remembrance lap in memory of Calyx and Beau: "If we turn this sad time into a joyful memory then their memory will live on through all of us." Parker stepped off the stage and took the first steps on the lap and, like the Pied Piper, he soon had many children following in his wake.

At eleven, the event was closed to the public and only the participants remained. Each of the school's fifty Relay For Life teams set up and decorated campsites to reflect their teams' names. Students sold food, drinks, and arts and crafts from the campsites day and night to continue their fundraising efforts.

Parker was part of it all. He took turns with the teams walking the track, laughed at the boys dressed in drag for the "S'He's so Hot" competition, and refereed dodgeball games, telling the competitors, "Just have fun, don't cheat, and if you hit the ref you're out."

The walks continued through the night. Calyx's friends embraced Parker as he walked, often hugging him so intently, they were forced to come to a halt as the other walkers had to flow around them. With a baseball cap on his head and a big smile on his face, Parker often progressed around the track with his arms around two and three kids at once.

Music that night started out sad and melancholy immediately after the remembrance ceremony, then gradually turned to a more energetic beat as Frisbee and Twister games broke out on the sidelines. At one point, Parker picked up a football, tossed it back and forth as he walked, and sang along with the popular songs.

On one pass of the Harry Potter tent, Parker said he had to read the series, because Calyx had said, "Dad, nerd is the word." Parker walked with his daughter's classmates until the sun rose. And then he walked some more—up until the end of the event at eight o'clock that morning.

At the closing ceremony, the winning team was announced—the Wizarding Independence Day team led the fund-raising effort in Calyx's name. Parker stepped back on the stage to accept the trophy in her honor.

CHAPTER 39

Julie's public defenders filed a motion to waive Julie's presence at the hearing to set deadlines on Tuesday, April 5, 2011. The motion was accepted and Julie was not present in the courtroom when the proceedings began at 8:30 that morning in front of Judge Ashley Moody.

The prosecution team was focused on harvesting data and evidence from the five computers recently seized from the Schenecker home. The defense attorneys were doing their best to squelch the flames of the intense media fires in the hopes of securing a fair trial for their client.

At the end of the hearing, their focus shifted to some degree because of the ruling from the bench. Judge Moody issued deadlines for both sides. The state had until August 15 to decide whether or not they would seek the death penalty. The defense had until then to announce if they would pursue an insanity defense.

On April 16, Parker attended a game played by a soccer team that once included Beau. Parker cheered on the sidelines and afterwards exchanged hugs with Beau's friends and classmates. These moments strengthened and comforted Parker and helped the children who knew Beau to heal from their shared pain.

* * *

That month, in response to Parker's request that the court determine a division of the couple's estimated $2 million in assets that was "unequal in his favor," Julie's divorce attorney, Ed Brennan, laid out her demands. First, he insisted that his client deserved a full half of the value of the savings, military pensions, vehicles, and three homes they owned in Tampa Palms, Maryland, and Kansas.

In addition, the document requested an immediate forty thousand dollars for a lawyer, ten thousand dollars for a forensic accountant, and permanent alimony and health coverage. Julie also requested a life insurance policy on Parker, naming her as the beneficiary, and the return of her diamond engagement ring.

Attorney Brennan also wanted the court to order an inventory of the contents of the house on Royal Park Court. He claimed that Parker was sending much of the family property to Texas, including Julie's personal items and jewelry.

Indeed, Parker was packing up the family's belongings in preparation for putting the house up for sale. His main concern was the school papers, report cards, track-and-field gear belonging to Calyx, and Beau's soccer trophies. He told *People* that he did not want to overlook a single scrap of paper: "I have to properly take care of things, for the kids. They were stolen away from me; they were stolen away from the world."

Parker also wanted the world to know that, although he traveled a lot, when he was at home he never missed a game or school event. "I was a connected dad," he said. "I was not one of those fathers who roll into a man cave."

In addition to the obvious reasons, Parker expressed a desire to leave the home because it was simply too big for one person. When *People* correspondent Steve Helling asked him how he felt about Julie that day, Parker took a contemplative pause before responding. "I feel for Julie," he said. "I'm going through my hell; she's going through her own hell. There's not hate in my heart. But there is no way I could see myself remaining married to her."

With his children gone and his wife behind bars Parker

was alone, but he was not lonely. He received more invitations to dinner from the military families at MacDill Air Force Base than he could handle. He received e-mail messages from other military facilities all over the world. He said that, other than changing his place of residence, he had no desire to start a new life, meet new people, or change anything in his life. He was intent on leading a life dedicated to the memory of his children, finding his comfort among old friends and the lasting alliances he had formed during his military career.

The exclusivity of this interview with a leading national magazine left local reporters wondering about how *People* managed to pull it off. Had they blurred the lines of journalistic ethics by making a donation to the Calyx and Beau Schenecker Foundation or with the purchase of photographs in exchange for this arrangement? Parker's public relations representative denied those possibilities when directly asked by *Tampa Bay Times* reporter Alexandra Zayas.

On May 6, an entity that delivered the headlines became part of the news. Media General, parent company of *The Tampa Tribune,* WFLA-TV, News Channel 8, and TBO, filed a motion in opposition to the temporary protective order filed by the defense. They wanted access to restricted information that they believed the public had a right to know.

CHAPTER 40

On May 9, Parker Schenecker filed his response to Julie's demands. He denied her request for alimony, calling it "unjust and inequitable," and requested that the court dissolve his marriage prior to the June date scheduled for the court battle. His attorney Alexander Caballero wrote that Parker "has tried to treat his Wife with a respect she declined to show her children but to remain married to the person that coldly executed his children would be morally repugnant to him."

Parker took another step in a different courtroom that day, filing a wrongful-death civil suit against his wife. The legal activity now hit a fever pitch with proceedings simultaneously occurring in criminal, civil, and divorce courts.

The document filed by the legal firm of Fonvielle Lewis Foote & Messer, of Tallahassee, began with a two-part complaint regarding the deaths of Parker's children and a request for an unspecified amount for damages. Following that was a twenty-seven-point statement of fact from the plaintiff's perspective that included the allegations that Julie's e-mails to Parker in Doha, Qatar, after the murders of Calyx and Beau were sent with "the intent or reckless disregard, to cause her husband severe emotional distress."

Then came the listing of counts, the first the intentional death or Beau; the second the deliberate killing of Calyx;

and finally the intentional infliction of emotional distress. In the latter section, Parker claimed that Julie's actions were "outrageous conduct . . . so outrageous, and so extreme in degree, as to go beyond all possible bounds of decency . . . and utterly intolerable in a civilized society."

In addition to the claims of severe distress caused to Parker by the acts of murder, the document further claimed that, in the death of Beau, "firing a shot through the windshield of the car created a sense of terror immediately prior to his death. Parker Schenecker's knowledge of his son's terror has caused him additional intensive emotional distress as a direct result of Julie Powers Schenecker's conduct."

Following the filing, Parker released a statement to the public:

> Today I have filed a wrongful death suit as well as other filings against my wife Julie for the murders of my children Calyx and Beau.
>
> This is a necessary step in my desire to give voice to my children and to ensure that throughout what may happen in the future criminal and civil litigation, Calyx and Beau are not forgotten.
>
> I feel strongly that Julie be held accountable for her selfish acts on January 27, 2011, when she silenced my children—I won't let that happen again. They deserve to be heard.
>
> I am choosing to file this suit to give voice to my children and to hold their murderer accountable for what she did. As I've said, my loss is total. But I won't let my children be silenced or forgotten now or ever.
>
> This is another step in my commitment to them, to my family and friends, their friends and to the public—to honor my kids and the way they lived. If I did not file this suit, I would not be true to my children or my character.
>
> I now look to the judicial system for help. It's a system I swore to protect and defend along with the U.S. Constitution for more than twenty-seven years in

uniform. I have faith in this system, that defends good over evil, will do the right thing and hold my children's murderer accountable for her actions.

In an interview with the *St. Petersburg Times* in the downtown riverfront of Tampa, he spoke of his fears that people would see his civil action as being all about money. He described the lawsuit as a mission that he was honor bound to complete and added that he wanted to use the couple's money to do good in the memory of their children: "I'm standing up for my kids . . . otherwise, I couldn't be the dad they knew."

He talked, too, of his future plans to end his army career by June and to find a smaller place to live near MacDill Air Force Base where he hoped to work as a civilian.

He was right to be concerned that many would see his filing as being about nothing more than money. Legal experts on the airways referred to the move as "smart lawyering" that was a strategy to recoup anything that Julie won in divorce court. The bottom line, though, was that Julie, like any spouse who gave up a career in the best interests of the family unit, did have grounds for her requests—and grounds that were even firmer for equitable distribution of funds from the sale of their primary home, and money in 401(k) and IRA accounts. Any alimony judgment could not be touched in a wrongful-death claim.

With the filing of the civil suit, Parker caused more lawyers to enter into Julie's universe of legal representation—seventy-nine-year-old Arnold Levine, with fifty years of experience, including defending Tampa Bay Buccaneers team members against murder charges; and Paul Sullivan, Levine's son-in-law, a former prosecutor with twenty-two years of experience as a defense attorney and qualified by the state supreme court to handle death penalty cases.

Immediately after joining the Julie Schenecker team, Levine announced that he would be taking over the criminal case as soon as Julie had access to funds: "The public defender is hanging in there right now because she doesn't have any property, money or assets."

Julie remained behind bars at the Falkenburg Road Jail, waiting for three different courts to decide her fate.

CHAPTER 41

On May 18, attorney Caballero, on Parker Schenecker's be-half, asked Hillsborough Circuit Judge Cheryl K. Thomas to order deputies to transport Julie from the county jail to her courtroom for questioning in the divorce matter. In no time, Julie's lawyer Ed Brennan filed an emergency motion to block that move.

He accused Parker of grandstanding and attempting to poison the potential jury pool for her upcoming criminal trial. Brennan also said that Julie had the right to avoid self-incrimination in that case and could not answer questions posed by her husband in the defense case for that reason.

Brennan also informed the court that his client was on a twenty-four-hour suicide watch in the infirmary at the jail and claimed that forcing her to attend a divorce hearing could damage her fragile mental health. Before the day was over, Julie agreed to the divorce, removing any need for an emotion-filled battle before Judge Thomas.

The next day, the divorce was finalized in five minutes and involved almost no discussion. Parker was there; Julie was not. The judge asked Parker, "Is your marriage irretriev-ably broken?"

Parker said, "Yes."

Judge Cheryl Thomas pounded a steel legal stamp on her order instantly dissolving the Scheneckers' twenty-year marriage: "From this day forward, you are considered divorced."

In divorce law, the judge invoked "bifurcation," which immediately ends the marriage but retains jurisdiction over future distribution of assets. Whatever the Scheneckers owned or saved in the marriage could not be touched by either party.

The judgment also granted Julie Schenecker the ability to restore her maiden name, but she would only be allowed to do that once—and then only after her criminal case had been closed.

The lawyers for both sides began work on a distribution of assets for the judge to review and approve. The legal minefield continued for Julie Schenecker. Three different courts still had control over her future. And the biggest obstacle to her continued existence rested in the hands of the criminal court. At this point, however, it was still not clear exactly what would be at stake at her upcoming trial and when that event would occur.

CHAPTER 42

On July 8, Julie was back in the courtroom. Her attorney, Robert Frasier, asked the judge to seal 23 of the 167 pages, as well as a number of photographs taken in the investigation, that the prosecution proposed to release. Included in what Frasier wanted excluded were writings by Julie that police found in her home and any description of the two dead teenagers, including their autopsy reports.

"I'm a little taken aback by the idea that we're all supposed to dance through the raindrops for Media General and the *St. Petersburg Times* when we have no duty to do that at all.

"I'm asking the court to take a hard look, a hard scrutiny, at these documents as Your Honor already has, I'm sure. I'd appreciate the significance to Julie Schenecker, if they were known to the community at large, regardless of whether they make it to the *St. Pete Times* or the *Tampa Tribune*. It's not their business. It's her business and it should stay there," Frasier argued.

"Case law is pretty clear that the court has a responsibility to balance the interests of the media. But first and foremost, I have to weigh the defendant's right to a fair trial and make sure she's afforded due process so I will give great consideration to each piece of discovery," Judge Moody responded.

Attorneys for Media General along with the *St. Petersburg Times* expressed their reasons for why they thought the items should not be blocked and asked the judge to make her ruling as lax as possible and still guarantee Julie's right to a fair trial. The judge released her decision four days later, ordering the State Attorney's Office to withhold the twenty-three pages as well as some photographs that the defense found objectionable and release the remaining materials to the public. On July 25, they did so, but they withheld some of the photographs in question.

After the materials were made available, Parker Schenecker made a statement saying that it was "another step in the judicial process." He added that the documents had "highlighted the substantial burden and responsibility that comes with access to details of my children's murders. My family, friends and I, along with the thousands who have mourned Calyx and Beau with us, will continue to honor my beautiful children, remembering them with dignity and respect."

Everyone was in court again on July 29, for the state to show cause why sanctions should not be imposed for a violation of the judge's July 12 order when it did not release eighty of the photographs. The prosecutors said that they were concerned about a new state law that made the depictions of the killing of a person exempt from public record.

Media attorney Gregg Thomas argued that the crime scene photographs should all be available for viewing because state law required the restriction of images of the actual killing, not photos from the crime scene taken a day later: "The photographs here are not of the killing—they're not of Julie Schenecker pulling a gun and killing her son and killing her daughter."

Calyx's friends made an event out of attending the opening showing of the seventh and final movie in the Harry Potter series, *Harry Potter and the Deathly Hallows—Part 2*. They all ached that Calyx could not be there with them, so they went to the film with thoughts of her and in her stead.

A Facebook page urged everyone to wear green attire in

general, Harry Potter gear, their rubber Calyx wristbands—
anything that indicated their support for Calyx. One hundred and sixty-one teenagers planned to do just that and go
to the midnight showing at Muvico in New Tampa as July 14
bled into July 15.

The most monumental announcement, since news of the
murder filtered out of Tampa Palms, arrived on Friday, August 12: Prosecutors submitted a terse statement that changed
the complexity and time line of the criminal proceedings:
"The State of Florida . . . gives notice to the defendant of the
State's intent to seek the death penalty for the murder of
Beau Powers Schenecker and Calyx Powers Schenecker."

Traditionally, it has been difficult for prosecutors to get a
death penalty sentence against any woman, and even more
challenging when that woman was white and middle-class.
Only 51 women have been executed in the United States
since 1900—compared to 8,879 men. In addition, jurors
have balked at deciding to give the most extreme punishment to women who kill their own children.

Florida, one of thirty-five states with the death penalty,
has shown no reluctance to enforce that sentence against
convicted male inmates. However, although thirty women in
Florida have been given a death sentence, to date only two
have actually had the penalty executed—the sentences of
the majority of the women were commuted to life.

The first was Judias Goodyear Buenoano, nicknamed
"The Black Widow." She was sentenced to death for the 1971
arsenic poisoning of her husband. She also received a life
sentence for the drowning murder of her paralyzed son in
1980. He was rendered a paraplegic after he'd been poisoned
with arsenic. She was also convicted of the 1983 attempted
murder of a fiancé and is suspected in the deaths of several
of her boyfriends. She died in the electric chair on March
30, 1998.

The second was Aileen Wuornos, in 2002, the first female to ever fit the FBI profile of a serial killer. She worked
as a prostitute and, on at least seven occasions, chose to

make money by killing and robbing her customers instead of or in addition to providing the agreed-upon services. She was convicted of murdering six of those men and received a death penalty sentence for each murder. She claimed that her victims had attempted to rape her and she only killed them in self-defense. She died of lethal injection on October 9, 2002.

For a while, Tiffany Cole was the only woman on Florida's Death Row. She went there in 2008 for the murders of a sixty-one-year-old couple, Carol and Reggie Sumner, whom Tiffany had buried alive after stealing their credit cards.

The three other women now on Death Row made their appearance there in 2011: Margaret Allen, for torturing and killing her housekeeper; Ana Maria Cardona, for the torture murder of her three-year-old son, the first time in twenty years that a Florida woman received the death penalty for the murder of her child; and Emilia Carr, for the kidnapping and murder of Heather Strong, the ex-wife of her co-defendant, and disposing of her body in a shallow grave beside a storage trailer.

Now Julie Schenecker faced the possibility of joining them on Death Row. Would her life be spared because of her social status, her military credentials, or her mental illness? Or would she become one of the small, infamous group of women sentenced to die for their crimes?

After receiving the decision from the prosecutors, Judge Ashley Moody gave the defense an additional five days to file their decision on whether or not they would pursue an insanity defense. Julie's attorneys must have seen it coming, because they were ready. They filed that same day.

The defense informed the judge that Julie could not discern between right and wrong when she shot her children on January 27: "She did not know what she was doing or its consequences. She did not know it was wrong and this was because the defendant was suffering from a mental infirmity, disease or defect, to wit: Bipolar Disorder with psychotic features."

Forty-six states—the exceptions being Utah, Montana, Idaho, and Kansas—allow some version of an insanity defense. The basis for most of these laws, including Florida's, is the M'Naghten Rule, named for a Scottish woodworker, Daniel M'Naghten. He traveled to 10 Downing Street in London with a plan to assassinate Prime Minister Robert Peel, because M'Naghten believed that he was a target of a conspiracy between the head of the British government and the pope. M'Naghten inadvertently killed the prime minister's secretary.

Several psychiatrists testified at his trial and M'Naghten was found not guilty by reason of insanity in 1843. An outraged public, which included Queen Victoria, led to the formation of a new legal standard: "In all cases that every man is to be presumed to be sane . . . until the contrary be proved . . . and that to establish a defense on the ground of insanity, it must be clearly proved that, at the time of the committing of the act, the party accused was labouring under such a defect of reason, from disease of the mind, as not to know the nature and quality of the act he was doing; or if he did know it, that he did not know he was doing what was wrong." In other words, acquittal was only possible if the defendant was mentally ill enough that he did not realize what he was doing was wrong.

In Florida, recent legislation has made the task of the defense in this plea even more onerous by the adoption of that presumption of sanity clause. This amendment shifted the burden of proof in a case like Julie Schenecker's from the prosecution to the defense, who are now required to demonstrate their client's insanity with "clear and convincing" evidence.

Many have questioned why we even need an insanity defense in the belief that all perpetrators should be treated the same in the courtroom. On her Fox TV show, Judge Jeanine Pirro said, "Insanity should not be used as an excuse for murder. It should only be considered in the sentencing phase after a verdict has been reached. At trial, the issue should be: Did she do it or didn't she? If yes, find her guilty and convict her, then deal with the mental illness in the penalty phase. If we don't and we turn our courts over to psychiatrists, we are then ruled by the laws of madness."

We do, however, already treat those who commit the same crime in different ways when we view their responsibility or reasoning to be diminished. For example, a child who accidentally started a fire will not be prosecuted as an arsonist, even though the damage done could have caused a multiple loss of lives. The insanity defense provides the same type of moral balance in the justice system by allowing judges and juries to determine whether or not the mentally ill defendant was as "criminally responsible" as someone who was without that organically disordered thinking.

Public perception has tended to be that the defense has been abused as a lame excuse for wrongdoing. To the contrary, the insanity plea has been entered in less than 1 percent of cases and acquittal has resulted in only 15 to 25 per cent of those cases.

Adding to the limitations of the possibility of success for an insanity defense has been the fear that the verdict would release the defendant back into society. Time and again, expert commentators have spoken of jurors' concerns about the societal cost of releasing a person back into the community when the individual's mental illness seemed to indicate a strong probability of a reoffense. Typically, however, the insanity determination has been the equivalent of a life sentence more often than not. M'Naghten himself died after twenty years in a mental asylum.

One thing was certain: Unless a plea bargain or some other event stopped the trial before it started, the clash would be epic. The death penalty, the most difficult prosecution goal to achieve, and the insanity defense, the least successful defense tactic, would do battle in a Florida courtroom for the life of Julie Schenecker.

CHAPTER 43

The favorite restaurant of Beau and Calyx Schenecker was the Grillsmith New American Grill in Wesley Chapel, beside the Shops at Wiregrass mall. Parker wanted to involve the restaurant in his fund-raising efforts for the Calyx and Beau Memorial Fund that he'd established through the Community Foundation of Tampa to recognize Bay area teenagers for their leadership, athleticism, and performing-arts abilities.

Parker approached Billy Grimm, the president of Grill-Smith, about planning something special for the six locations in the Tampa Bay area. Billy agreed and they designed the Back to School Week fund-raiser in memory of the two children. School started on Tuesday, August 23, that year, and the event ran seven full nights, from Monday through Sunday.

GrillSmith decided to donate 100 percent of the proceeds from the sale of Calyx's favorite dish, Caribbean Pumpkin Crab Bisque soup, "rich and creamy with toasted almonds and a dollop of cream," and Beau's favorite appetizer, Spicy Thai Shrimp, "lightly battered, flash-fried shrimp tossed in sriracha aioli, served with a hot and sweet honey glaze." Billy Grimm announced the plans and said that by donating all proceeds from the kids' favorites at GrillSmith to their memorial fund "we not only bring awareness to the fund itself but also shine a light on the two amazing kids that, quite frankly, were taken away too soon."

Parker added his comments to the announcement, too:

Calyx and Beau were devoted friends, classmates and teammates. They were everything a parent could ever ask for—responsible, loving and connected to those around them. Both were model citizens, standouts in the classroom and on the sports fields, and big fans of GrillSmith. My family and I would like to thank Grill-Smith for their generosity and support. Relationships were ultimately important to Calyx and Beau and this opportunity along with friends to celebrate the lives of my exceptional children will be a fitting tribute to them. Calyx and Beau would be so humbled and honored by the generosity of so many.

The event kicked off Monday night with a small group of teachers, principals, and students who knew Calyx and Beau gathered in a private room at the location both children liked to visit near their home. Parker was the host and his mother, Nancy Schenecker, was there to assist and honor her grandchildren.

No one mentioned the horrible way that Calyx and Beau died. No one even whispered Julie Schenecker's name. At Parker's insistence, it was a celebration of his son's and daughter's lives: "Your presence tonight states a lot to us. It tells me your continued love for two people who I know loved you and you know loved you."

Saturday night was King High Day at the GrillSmith near the Shops at Wiregrass mall. It was a busy time for the staff at the restaurant as Caribbean Pumpkin Crab Bisque soup and Spicy Thai Shrimp flew out of the kitchen.

Throughout the weeklong event, the six GrillSmith restaurants served 885 orders of Calyx's favorite soup and 938 orders of Beau's favorite appetizer, raising $10,500 for the memorial fund. "It is our privilege to be able to help in whatever way we can," Billy Grimm said. "Our hearts certainly go out to the entire Schenecker family who are trying to heal from this tragedy. . . . Thank you to all who came out to support the memorial fund and celebrate Calyx and Beau's lives."

If life had gone on as it should have done, Calyx would have celebrated her seventeenth birthday on September 12, 2011. Her friend Sara Wortman repeated her actions from the year before, bringing red velvet cupcakes that she and her mother baked to school in honor of Calyx's special day.

On September 29 that year, Beau would have celebrated his fourteenth birthday. In honor of that day, Parker wrote a brief poem to his son, which he later shared on tribute Internet sites. He wrote that his son was missed by many and that he was proud to have been his father. He figuratively gave him "A box of 14 Krispy Kremes with a bow on it." The last line of the poem harkened back to wonderful memories of their time together: "I love you son, Infinity + 1." He signed it, "Love, Daddio."

CHAPTER 44

On December 5, 2011, Ed Brennan and Arnold Levine filed a response to the civil case brought by Parker against their client Julie. In the first section of the complaint Brennan and Levine admitted the jurisdictional scope of the court and the paternity of both children but denied Parker's role overseeing the estates of Calyx and Beau and asserted Julie's Fifth Amendment privilege to not issue an answer about the way the two died.

In the statement of facts, Julie agreed to the first two regarding her and Parker's military service and marriage but denied that she and Parker agreed that Julie leave the army "to nurture and raise their children" and that he would make a career in the army.

She claimed to have no knowledge of Parker's military career, his deployments, and the need that created to relocate the family on several occasions. She acknowledged that the couple had purchased a home in Tampa but denied the agreement on which home to buy. She also denied that she and the children communicated with him by telephone during his recent absence.

She again claimed Fifth Amendment protection for the facts relating to the purchase of the gun and the deaths of her children. She denied speaking to Parker on the telephone on January 24 or 25 and claimed no knowledge of the e-mail he sent about his arrival in Qatar or of his actions after the children had died.

As to the counts filed in the suit, she claimed privilege on most points and, in addition, denied any knowledge of Parker's emotional distress. At the conclusion of that section, Julie demanded that "the Plaintiff take nothing by virtue of the complaint" and that she be awarded "the reasonable costs incurred by her in connection with the defense of the suit to date."

The affirmative defense claims followed. The first one asserted that Julie "by reason of a mental disease and defect, did not know the nature or consequences of her actions and was incapable of distinguishing that which is right from that which is wrong."

Then, the bomb dropped.

In her second affirmative defense, the document cited the "contributory negligence of Parker Schenecker." Julie alleged that any damages suffered by her husband "were proximately caused by Plaintiff's own negligence, both individually or as a beneficiary, [and] should be either barred or diminished in accordance with the degree of Plaintiff's own negligence." Parker, she claimed, bore responsibility because he left her "alone to care for their children . . . even though he was fully aware that . . ." she "had suffered for many years from mental disease or defect."

Following that claim, the document iterated the history of Julie's marriage from her initial diagnosis during the year they were married, through all the occasions of hospitalization, drugs, and mental health treatment, to the expanded diagnosis ten years later. It stated that Parker further demonstrated his awareness of her diminished capabilities when, less than two weeks before the deaths of Calyx and Beau, he sent an e-mail to the family describing Julie as having "the judgment of a 10-year-old."

The document concluded with a damning statement:

Because of Parker Schenecker's knowledge of Julie Powers Schenecker's mental infirmities, and because of their relationship as husband and wife, and as parents, Parker Schenecker owed a duty of care to Julie Powers Schenecker, Beau Schenecker and Calyx Schenecker, to see that Julie Powers Schenecker received proper care for her condition and infirmities. Parker Schenecker breached this duty by leaving Julie Powers Schenecker and his children all alone while he traveled overseas, thereby, by his conduct, creating a foreseeable zone of risk and harm to his children.

After the filing, attorney Paul Sullivan told the *St. Petersburg Times* that they had hoped to not file a response until much later "to keep from riling up all the hard feelings," but Julie needed to put up a defense:

It was our sad duty to point how seriously mentally ill Mrs. Schenecker had been for so many years. . . . All through his marriage, he relied on people to help when she's been bad off, but this time he didn't. . . . It was partially negligence on his part that led to these children being left alone with their mother at a time when the dad, according to his own emails, could clearly tell she was a danger to herself and others. . . . At a period when she was perhaps at the very worst she'd ever been, he just left the country and took zero action to have anybody around to look after the children and look after Ms. Schenecker.

The bluntness of his next comment shocked many: "He sued his wife for divorce and sued his wife for wrongful death. It's regrettable to come to this, but our position's quite simply had he done something to help his wife in her hour of need, his children may not be dead now."

Lawyer Ed Brennan, speaking to the *Tampa Tribune*, added: "If it is determined that Julie has liability for the wrongful death of those children, then Mr. Schenecker has some culpability for the death of those children. . . . Why would you leave her alone? Nobody knows why he did what he did. . . . He had a drowning situation and rather than throwing her a life preserver he threw her an anchor."

Parker's spokesperson dismissed the accusations from Julie's civil suit legal team in a new statement release:

> *While not surprised at Mrs. Schenecker's response yesterday, Mr. Schenecker will continue to hold his ex-wife responsible for her horrific actions when she murdered their children last January. He remains undeterred in his efforts to forever honor Calyx and Beau's memories through the foundation he created just days after their deaths. By court filing, it confirms Mrs. Schenecker would prefer to point the finger of blame at others while invoking her Fifth Amendment right. Mr. Schenecker is simply seeking justice to be served for his children and that their murderer be held responsible for her actions. So that he can truly focus on honoring the way they lived and by spending his time involved in things that were important to them.*

* * *

The attack on Parker's image did not send him into hiding. Ten days after the filed document became public, Parker appeared for a special presentation at Liberty Middle School.

The student body, led by the efforts of the National Junior Honor Society and the Future Business Leaders of America groups at the school, had raised two thousand dollars that fall selling Butter Braid pastry. With Parker's promised matching donation, it brought the total of their contribution to the foundation to four thousand dollars.

About a hundred students attended, many far more dressed up than they would be for classes, along with school officials for the presentation for the oversized facsimile of a check. Parker was obviously moved. He had to pause during speaking to collect the overflow of his emotions. "Just remember that they are here with you. I cannot thank you enough." Before he could finish, Parker's voice cracked. After clearing his throat, he continued, "Let's hope 2012 has calmer seas."

Parker left the ceremony with a difficult period of time lying ahead of him. In ten days it would be Christmas—the first Christmas in twenty years that he had no spouse by his side and no children bouncing with eager, energetic anticipation of the special day. The anniversary of two loved ones' deaths, the one Parker would face in a month and a half, the birth dates of those deceased, but often most of all the Christmas holidays—these were land mines awaiting anyone in the throes of grief, and the first time they were experienced was the most challenging of all. Parker had to face his first experience with the holidays in December and then the first anniversary of his children's deaths in January. It was not an ordeal anyone would envy.

CHAPTER 45

The advertisement for the house at 16305 Royal Park Court read: "Tampa Palms Beauty! Move-in ready. NOT a short-sale. Can close quickly." It did not mention the tragedy that occurred there in January 2011. Although many people would consider it a material fact, something that would affect the buyer's decision to purchase or the price offered, existing Florida law demanded that a murder committed in the home did not need to be revealed unless a direct question was asked.

Stigmatized properties, like the Schenecker home, have had a long history of difficulty on the real estate market. The Clutter home, depicted in Truman Capote's book *In Cold Blood*, may never sell at full value. The nine-thousand-square-foot villa with a swimming pool and private tennis courts where thirty-nine members of the Heaven's Gate cult drank vodka-and-barbiturate cocktails to end their lives in order to ascend to a spaceship riding along with the Hale-Bopp comet was valued at $1.6 million. When the owner could not move the property he gave it back to the bank. The bank sold it for just $668,000. After the sale, bulldozers moved in and demolished the home.

In Colorado, the home where JonBenét Ramsey lived and died continued to be a white elephant on the market. Family members were the initial suspects after the death of the little girl on December 26, 1996, but even after they were cleared of any role in the crime the house remained tainted.

Forensic psychiatrist Park Dietz told *USA Today,* "People are superstitious. They're afraid of bad luck or ghosts or that the house is cursed. Or they have a more rational concern that the tragedies will be more salient to them. It may be on their consciousness and decrease their joy in living."

That is one reason that some murder houses do not make it to the marketplace. In 1979, John Gacy's house, in Norwood Park Township outside of Chicago, where he hid the bodies of twenty-nine of victims in the walls and crawl space, was totally demolished as law enforcement searched for every possible corpse. Nonetheless, even the empty lot sat unwanted for years before someone finally built a new house on it in 1988.

Nearer to the Schenecker home, in Homosassa, the mobile home where John Couey raped and held Jessica Lunsford captive for three days was destroyed nine days before the fourth anniversary of Jessica's abduction. It burned to the ground in a fire deemed suspicious by Citrus County officials.

In St. Petersburg, just three days before Julie murdered her children, Hydra Lacy Jr. shot at police officers Jeffrey Yaslowitz and Thomas Batinger and a federal agent before killing himself. Yaslowitz and Batinger died from their injuries. Mayor Bill Foster ordered the demolition of the home because of both the health and safety issues it created as well as the desire to obliterate the constant reminder of the community's loss.

When a traumatic event like murder reverberated in the media, the sale often took a long time and reduced a home's value by up to 25 percent. Overlay that fact with the down real estate market in Florida and Parker had a major challenge on his hands in his attempt to unload the family property.

All things considered, he did very well. A home he paid $448,000 for in 2008, which was valued at $261,000 in 2010, was purchased by Anthony and Christine Betts, in late 2011, for $385,000, just a bit over its estimated worth.

CHAPTER 46

As if there were not enough distractions for the multiple courts involved in the Schenecker tragedy, another roadblock was revealed in the criminal proceedings on January 18, 2012. The state digital forensic lab had pulled ninety-three discs of data from the computers in the home. Both the prosecutor and the defense received full copies of these DVDs, but neither could read the data contained on them. By law, the state needed to provide all the evidence they had to the defendant—and when the formatting made the material unintelligible it was the equivalent of withheld information.

The development bothered Judge Ashley Moody, who said, "My concern is in this new age of electronic data we're not giving the defense so much data that it's unsearchable." She gave both sides an additional forty-five days to work on the problem, ordering them back to court on March 14 with progress reports.

The state planned to process the data in-house using En-Case, the software for digital forensics that has been used by authorities across the country. The public defender's office did not have access to that program or the staffing needed to extract the material or the funds required for both the previous requirements to perform that task themselves. They had no recourse but to turn it all over to a private firm to decipher.

Before dismissing the court session, the judge reminded the state, "The defense needs data that is searchable and understandable."

The March date came and went without any progress. Everyone gathered back in front of Judge Moody on May 31. The judge wanted a strategy and time line. Julie's attorneys were discouraging about the progress of the exploration of the contents of the computer. They complained about the seemingly infinite number of e-mails, searches, Facebook interactions, and miscellaneous items retrieved from the computers in the Schenecker household.

The judge cut to the chase, asking the defense how many of the items they had read to date.

Assistant Public Defender Robert Frasier said, "I read several this morning."

Judge Moody was clearly disturbed. "This morning? It's been five months and you cannot even tell me what you've got?"

"This is completely unprecedented. The manpower needed is almost impossible to predict," Frasier said.

"You tell me you just started looking this morning," Moody chastised. "We need to make this a priority. Please put manpower on it. Put in the time that's necessary." She then ordered the defense and the prosecution to report back to her on July 12 about the data that they felt needed to be blocked from public release. She reminded both sides, "Deadlines are not requests. They are orders."

In early August, the judge finally had an answer to the volume of data in the five Schenecker computers. "The defense estimates 1,140,087 files will take approximately 2,071 hours or 51.78 weeks."

Judge Moody granted the Public Defenders' Office one year to complete their review. No one knew, though, if it would be worth the effort. Would anything of evidentiary value be uncovered in the data? Would there be any new material that would further the state's case or add to mitigating circumstances for the defense?

* * *

The one-year anniversary of the deaths of Calyx and Beau Schenecker arrived on Friday, January 27, 2012. The evening before, Betsey Giammattei uploaded a video of "Strange Little Running Girl," with lyrics by Jacob Gassen and the music she had composed. The visual part of the presentation included illustrations created by Calyx's good friend Jena Young. Beneath the screen, Betsey wrote: "It's been a year, and a long year at that. We miss you both every day. Prayers go out to the Schenecker family, especially you, Mr. Parker. We love you so much and are amazed at your incredible strength. . . . This one's for Calyx and Beau and your Harry Potter, running love."

On the anniversary day, students arrived at King High School wearing Harry Potter clothing and accessories or the color green for Calyx's love of Slytherin. Others showed up at Liberty Middle School and Freedom High School, which Beau would have attended that year had he lived, wearing Beau's favorite color, blue, or clad in soccer gear.

Dr. Kirsh was still seeing children traumatized by the event one year later. The potential for the delayed onset of PTSD was there for all of the children. She knew some of the kids would have lifelong chronic anxiety as the result of what had happened. She also knew that some of them would have such serious trust issues that they may limit themselves for the rest of their lives.

She had one patient who was suicidal and still not functioning well a full year after the murders. One little third-grade girl told Dr. Kirsh shortly after the anniversary, "I'm just afraid that my mother will get so angry with me and she'll hurt me. Sometimes she drinks and I get scared that she will crack."

All young hearts broken by a loss they could not understand and never would forget.

Since the turn of the century, the Dale Mabry Campus of Hillsborough Community College has displayed an exhibition of artwork executed by high school students. The 2012 show opened on April 12 with a permanent change in its name. A donation from the Calyx and Beau Memorial Foundation ensured that it would now be known as "Calyx Schenecker Art Infinitum" in honor of the young artist who lost her life at the age of sixteen.

One hundred and eighty students submitted their art into competition for twenty-five hundred dollars in award prizes. Parker made the selection of Calyx's works for the exhibition brochure, choosing those that represented "a period in her life when she was specifically delighted and fascinated by Asian culture."

In August and September of 2012, Parker and Grillmasters repeated the previous year's event at the restaurants to raise money for the Calyx and Beau Memorial Fund. In November, the Future Business Leaders of America and the National Junior Honor Society paired up to conduct a cookie dough fundraiser. They surpassed their goal of $5,000, netting $6,000 for the foundation. In less than two years, the memorial fund had received $92,000 in contributions and had awarded twelve scholarships.

Everyone waited to see when and if this case would actually go to trial. A full-blown proceeding is not an inevitability. A plea bargain that would eliminate days of testimony and argument continues to be a very real possibility. Barring a deal between the state and the defense, an epic battle will ensue between advocacy of the ultimate punishment of death and an argument against Julie's legal responsibility because of mental and emotional defects that demonstrate her insanity. In this situation, it will be difficult to select a jury and those chosen will need to make a decision that could haunt them for the rest of their lives.

Finally, in December 2012, Judge Moody set a trial date for October 7, 2013, but since death penalty cases often take two to three years until the final reckoning in the courtroom, another delay is not inconceivable. The judge also ordered lawyers on both sides to provide the court, by late January, a schedule detailing the public release of the voluminous data files.

A plea agreement prior to a trial would serve family members and friends well—it would end the anguish of the unknown and enable them to move on with their lives and would definitely save the taxpayers money. It may possibly be the best solution for both legal teams, the families, and the community involved in this heartrending tragedy.

Sitting on the sidelines while this legal wrangling continues are two parents who have lost their children. While Julie Schenecker stares at the blank walls and forbidding bars of a jail cell what thoughts run through her head? Remorse? Regret? Guilt? Or does she still believe she was justified in her actions? If anyone knew, it was Julie. But with her fragile mental health did she even understand her own responsibility?

The other parent, Parker Schenecker, deals with his own demons. He carries the burden of contemporary America's approach to death. Unlike the Israelis' and other cultures, he did not set aside his normal life with an intense, proscribed period of official grieving, designed to start the healing process. Instead, he soldiers on with the "celebration of life" approach—a candy-coated denial of the reality of the loss where wailing and gnashing of teeth is suppressed for expressions of joy of having known the deceased while they lived.

Like most men, Parker felt responsible for protecting his family. Fathers everywhere have been consumed by guilt when tragedy befell their wife or their children—even in cases where there was no indication of anything amiss, even when the damage done was the result of an accident or illness. So how much heavier is that burden for Parker? He knew his wife was not mentally stable. He knew there was conflict between his children and their mother. He could have felt his decisions and actions cleared the way for the deaths of the children. But what if he had reached a different decision? What if he'd not deployed overseas? Would his children still be alive? Or would Julie have found another way to end the lives of Calyx and Beau? Determined people have always been capable of overcoming obstacles in their paths. There very well may have been nothing Parker could have done to prevent this calamitous event.

At this point in time, the players are all gathered on the stage for the final act to begin, while the public waits for the curtains to open. No matter what the outcome in a case like this one, where emotions have run so high and answers have been so few, there will be no consensus on that outcome—no possible conclusion that can do justice to the family and friends of Beau and Calyx Schenecker.

AFTERWORD

When any mother kills her child, it is an attack on our pre-
conceived notions of motherhood. Contrary to everything
we intuitively expect from the mother-child bond, this crime
is not as rare as we would like to believe. According to
forensic psychologist Geoffrey R. McKee, author of *Why
Mothers Kill,* "biological mothers account for 30% of all
child homicides between 1976 and 2000 at an annual rate as
high as 256 or, on average, one child every thirty-three hours."

More conservative estimates, like that of Cheryl Meyer
and Michelle Obermann, co-authors of *Mothers Who Kill
Their Children*, place the incidence of these crimes at one
hundred times a year, making it every three days that a
mother kills a child in the United States. Even as one reads
about the prevalence of the crime in these statistics, it remains difficult to comprehend how any woman could carry
a developing fetus in her body for nine months and not feel
the intensity of the maternal bond that would prevent such
an act. Our reluctance as a society to believe that mothers
would be capable of killing their offspring hinders our ability to recognize warning signs, intervene, and prevent more
tragedies.

When I researched the history of mothers who kill, the
murders committed by Julie Schenecker grew even less
comprehensible—they are clearly an anomaly in the litera-

ture. Dr. Phillip Resnick, professor of psychiatry at Case Western Reserve University of Medicine and noted maternal filicide expert, commented in the first week following the crime, "It is very puzzling. You might expect a parent to lose control and smack the kids, not come up from behind with a gun. There is something else going on that we don't know about. On its face, it just doesn't compute." Even the ages of Calyx and Beau made the circumstances unusual—85 percent of the victims of maternal filicide are under six years of age.

The two most common acts of maternal filicide are neonaticide, a term coined by Resnick in 1970 and defined as the killing of a newborn less than twenty-four hours old; and infanticide, the killing of a baby less than one year of age. Resnick said that the most likely time to be killed by a parent is on the day the child is born. This crime is committed most commonly by teenage mothers who are alone and unattended by any medical personnel when they give birth. New mothers under fifteen are seven times more likely to commit neonaticide or infanticide than new mothers over the age of twenty-five.

Mental illness is a big factor in these cases, but so is desperation. Desperation often leads to denial of the pregnancy and to an overwhelming fear that parents or others in authority would learn about the birth.

The denial takes two forms. In one, the mother-to-be does not accept the fact that she is pregnant and no physical evidence of her condition will convince her. The mother can even walk away from the birth itself with no conscious awareness that she left a baby behind. In affective denial, the mother accepts the reality of the pregnancy on an intellectual level but does not feel the normal emotions of a woman in that state. She does not inform anyone, see a physician, or make any preparations for the arrival of a child—definitely not the normal behavior of the first-time mother, who often obsesses about the coming child.

E. L. Atkins argued in the *American Journal of Forensic Psychology* that those who kill infants in the first twenty-four hours of their life usually commit the act without any premeditation, acting in a state of impulsive panic, and thus are no threat to society, making incarceration unwarranted. Across the nation, a study discovered that only twenty-nine out of forty-two mothers who caused their newborn's death were charged with homicide. Often lesser charges like the unlawful disposal of a body were all the other women faced. In the punishment phase, the sentences handed down ranged from parenting classes and counseling to thirty years behind bars.

In the United States, all these cases have been approached as homicides from the onset because there are no specific neonaticide or infanticide laws here. Thirty other nations, including Turkey, England, India, Sweden, and Brazil, have laws targeting this specific crime. Great Britain passed the Infanticide Act of 1922—ninety years ago. British law works on the assumption that a woman who kills a newborn is most likely mentally unbalanced, and thus it prohibits prosecutors from placing any charge higher than manslaughter.

In 1994 France struck down their infanticide statute, and the French now charge the mothers based on the homicide laws. There may not be any connection, but France now has a rising number of these crimes and has the highest rates of neonaticide in Europe.

Less common is the murder of a child when its role in the family has been firmly established. In 1990, Patricia Crittenden and S. Craig determined that the proportion of children killed by parents decreased as the child grew older.

Resnick created the first classification system for this rarer form of maternal filicide, basing it on the mother's motivation. The first category is altruistic killings. Within that grouping are two subsets. In one are the cases where a mother commits a mercy killing, taking the life of a child who is suffering with a debilitating disease. The second contains mothers who believe that killing their offspring is in the best interests of those children.

In some cases, the mother plans to commit suicide but does not want to abandon her children. She reasons that by taking their lives she can protect them by keeping them by her side in heaven. "The mother may well think of young children as extensions of herself and feel that her children would be lost without her," Phillip Resnick told *Time* magazine. This motivation was evident in the cases of Kristina Gaime and Dorothy Ross in the Tampa Bay area.

In others, the mother wants to save her child from an even worse fate than death. Andrea Yates is a prime example of this irrational thinking. She drowned all five of her children one-by-one in the bathroom of her Clearwater, Texas, home, then calmly waited for the police. She believed she was saving her children from the devil. Her mental illness was the obvious cause of that dreadful conclusion, but proving Andrea's insanity would prove tricky—it took two trials. In most states, the legal definition requires that a perpetrator cannot distinguish between right and wrong, but Andrea walked a fine line. She believed killing her children was secularly wrong but simultaneously believed that it was right in God's eyes. Like most women who commit altruistic filicide, an element of disordered thinking was behind her actions, even though her thinking did not fit the legal definition of insanity.

Julie Schenecker, on the other hand, has not spoken of any lofty motivations for the murders of Calyx and Beau.

Resnick's second classification is the unwanted child filicide, not including those in the separate neonaticide category. This motivation revolves around illegitimacy or questions about paternity. These children die from either passive neglect or active, abusive aggression. Also included in this category are mothers who wanted the child initially but after the baby was born grow detached, resentful, or worn-out from the responsibility.

This reason has never been shown to exist in cases where the children were older, more independent, and better equipped to care for themselves. It is not a category where Julie Schenecker would comfortably fit. When she was not in a depressive state, she was an energetic and creative mother.

The third category is accidental filicide. Generally, these are cases of battering mothers who, in an attempt to discipline, engage in a fatal assault without any preplanning. These deaths typically follow a long history of child abuse.

Julie is surely not one of these mothers. Her only resorts to the physical abuse of her children were two slapping incidents involving her daughter just months prior to the murders. In addition, Julie engaged in premeditation. Not only did she travel away from her home turf to buy a gun, but after making that purchase and learning of the five-day waiting period she also came home and wrote: "The massacre will have to be delayed." Then, throughout what could have been a cooling-off period, she maintained her resolve and did not alter her plan.

Also included in this category are the cases of Munchausen syndrome by proxy, where the mother is intentionally harming the child to gain attention from medical professionals but has no intention of actually ending that child's life.

Resnick's next category, retaliation/spousal revenge filicide, is the result of a breakdown in a relationship that arouses the negative emotional reactions of jealousy or rejection. Often, a spouse's infidelity is the triggering mechanism for this class of murder. It is also possible that the affection that the other spouse received from the child was internalized as a threat to the marital sexual relationship. Resnick posited that this parent's homicidal impulse toward the child was a deliberate attempt to make the other parent suffer. It could also be present when a parent feels rejected by the child because of abuse or illness.

Here is a category that theoretically could be a motivation for Julie Schenecker. Did she feel threatened by the relationship one or both of her children had with Parker? Did she feel rejected by her children—by Calyx in particular? It clearly seems possible that those thoughts were in Julie's mind. Parker, in his civil suit, made it clear that he believed resentment was present in the e-mail she sent to him right after she killed the children. When she wrote: "Get home soon—we're waiting for you!" was she giving a clear indication of a desire to inflict severe emotional distress on her husband, as Parker's lawsuit claimed? Or was it another symptom of the disordered thinking of mental illness?

The catch is that this motivation is more likely to be found in paternal filicide. "Filicides based on retaliation and on jealousy or rejection almost exclusively involved fathers," McKee wrote. In every case I could find where a mother fit into this category, it was born from the belief that another adult was attempting to take the mother's child or children away from her.

Although it still remains a possibility, there was much more behind Julie Schenecker's actions, making her fall most readily into Resnick's fifth and final category: mental illness. Studies have demonstrated that 80 percent of mothers who commit filicide had a documented psychiatric history. P. T. d'Orbán researched the most common diagnoses of these mothers. Leading the pack at 43 percent of mentally ill women killing their children was the indication of a personality disorder.

Personality disorder is one of the diagnoses in Julie's mental health records. Psychologically, "personality" refers to the lasting behaviors and mental traits that distinguish one human being from another. A disorder of the personality indicates that the experiences and actions of the individual deviate from what is acceptable to society, causing disruption in the person's social and personal life. These disorders are consistent with the individual's sense of self and as such are deemed normal and appropriate to the person possessing them, causing anxiety, distress, depression, or all of the above.

The second most common diagnosis, at 21 percent, is acute reactive depression, a transitory condition that is brought on by environmental factors or circumstances such as grief. Julie's mental state went beyond this diagnosis to major depressive disorder, diagnosed nearly twenty years before the deaths of her children.

Defined as having feelings of sadness, loss, anger, discouragement, or frustration that disrupt a person's life for weeks or longer at a time, a major depression is demonstrated in a range of symptoms: agitation, restlessness, and irritability; dramatic change in appetite often with weight gain or loss; extreme difficulty in concentrating; fatigue or lack of energy; feelings of hopelessness and helplessness; feelings of worthlessness, self-hate, and guilt; becoming withdrawn or isolated; loss of interest or pleasure in activities that were once enjoyed; thoughts of death or suicide; and/or trouble sleeping or excessive sleeping.

There is no doubt that Julie was afflicted with many of these problems. And depression is a common precursor to the act of filicide, particularly in cases where there is a planned suicide component. One mother in four who kill their children successfully commits suicide. Many more try and some grow so emotionally exhausted by the act of taking the lives of their children that they lack the energy to go through with the final part of their plan.

Julie had clearly stated her intentions with regard to suicide. Her journal made it clear that after killing her children she planned on taking her own life. Did she think she'd taken a lethal cocktail of medications that night? Did she totally exhaust her ability to take any additional action to complete her plan by ending her own life, too?

Complicating Julie's mental health was her later diagnosis of bipolar disorder, also known as manic-depressive illness, responsible for unusual shifts in mood, energy, and the ability to carry out the tasks of everyday life. People with this disorder experience intense mood episodes that range from an overly joyful or overexcited state, a manic episode, to an extremely hopeless state, a depressive episode, as well as the possibility of a long-lasting unstable mood that isn't easily broken down into separate mania and depressive episodes. Julie's downs seemed to dominate, but Parker's references to times when she was not compliant with her medication made it clear that there were episodes of mania in her life. The inappropriate clothing choices Julie made in the last week of the children's lives was also indicative of a manic state.

Substance abuse is also very common among people with bipolar disorder—which was a major source of the turmoil in Julie's inner life. According to the Mayo Clinic Web site, "some people with bipolar disorder may try to treat their symptoms with alcohol or drugs. However, substance abuse may trigger or prolong bipolar symptoms, and the behavioral control problems associated with mania can result in a person drinking too much."

Bipolar disorder can cause angry behavior, energy levels that range from incredibly high to nonexistent, increased risk taking, and even feelings of creativity and mystical experience. Julie's fascination with how the writings of Tolle made her see everything in a new way was possibly an outgrowth of her mania.

Although delusions, fixed, false, irrational, or illogical beliefs, and hallucinations, hearing, seeing, or sensing things for which there is no physical stimulus, are most frequently seen in manic states, the delusions are also apparent in severe melancholic depression in people with bipolar disorder. The types of delusions include both grandiose—making people believe they possess special gifts or power that others don't have or that they have access to information that is hidden to others—and persecutory, a belief that people are out to get them or that something bad is about to happen.

Writer Sylvia Plath, who is believed to have had bipolar disorder, wrote before her suicide at the age of thirty: "It is as if my life were magically run by two electric currents: joyous positive and despairing negative—whichever one is running at the moment dominates my life, floods it. I am now flooded with despair, almost hysteria, as if I were smothering. As if a great muscular owl were sitting on my chest, its talons clenching and constricting my heart."

Coming in third in d'Orbán's list of common mental illnesses in mothers who kill their children was psychotic illness at 16 percent. Julie Schenecker's diagnosis of schizoaffective disorder put her in this category, too. It is a condition with symptoms of both schizophrenia and bipolar disorder. Take the bipolar symptoms listed earlier and add to the mix disorganized thinking, odd or unusual behavior, slow movements or total immobility, lack of emotion in facial expression and speech, and poor motivation. It is a chaotic and unstable affliction that creates an unimaginably difficult way of life.

Forensic psychologist Geoffrey McKee added a sixth category to the list of motivations at the root of mothers killing children: psychopathic killers. These women have dark, sinister reasons for their behavior, often killing their children or allowing others to do so for their own personal gain. These women kill for insurance money or turn their children over to sexual predators in exchange for the drugs to feed the mother's habit. Some of them were victims of childhood neglect or abuse and inflict the same torment on their own children with glee.

Julie Schenecker does not fit into this category, although the prosecution would probably like it if the jury saw her that way. She does not display the aggressive narcissism present in a psychopath; friends described her as quiet and elegant. She did not have the socially deviant lifestyle stretching back to the teenage years that is the hallmark of these individuals. She did not have any of the other traits commonly seen in psychopathology: promiscuous sexual behavior, many short-term marital relationships, or criminal versatility.

In addition to the multiplicity of mental illnesses afflicting Julie, she also suffered from tardive dyskinesia, a permanent Parkinson's-like disease brought on by some psychoactive medications. The condition causes sudden, uncontrollable movements of voluntary muscle groups in the facial features and in the limbs. Because of that, she had to deal with the fact that her body was now betraying her just as her mind had been doing for years.

Many people, including Julie's defense team, wonder why Parker did not see the red flags of danger and take action. Looking back, we find it far easier to determine what we could have done differently to ensure a better outcome.

Parker, however, did not have a crystal ball, and living in the moment he did not believe that his wife would kill their children. A lot of people placed in his position would not have assumed the worst, either. Certainly he was aware of the presence of some fear in his children. He wrote to Julie: "They've asked their father for protection. The hard part of this is that they've asked for protection from their mother."

In an e-mail to his family, he referred to his wife as having the judgment of a ten-year-old, but he had no way of knowing exactly what thoughts were racing through his wife's mind. Maybe if he had been able to get feedback from her psychiatrist Parker would have been better prepared to protect his children.

HIPAA regulations stood in the way of him obtaining that information. Are the rules too rigid? Not having them in place opens up an enormous possibility of abuse and misuse of the material by a spouse without the best interests of a partner in their hearts. In this case, though, it appears as if it could have made a positive difference that could have saved the children's lives. Their ability to change the outcome depended on how much Julie's mental health professionals knew and how well they assessed the risks of the danger that Julie presented to those around her.

How can we help these mothers and prevent these crimes in the future? Experts have many specific suggestions for the prevention of neonaticide and infanticide. They even have many warnings and recommendations for proactive interference when risk factors are present. However, it is not always as easy to see or as easy to accomplish when older children are endangered by their mothers.

The most important thing we can do is make mental health services more accessible and more effective for everyone. Because of the cases of death as a result of systematic child abuse or neglect, we need to take every single instance of violence against a child seriously—even when the injury itself is not serious. Neither of those things will eliminate filicide, but they would go a long way toward limiting the numbers.

Perhaps the biggest part of the solution is for our society to develop a better understanding and acceptance of mental illness. We often expect people with depression, panic attacks, or psychotic thinking to pull themselves together, to snap out of it, to shape up—not a reasonable expectation. In the grip of the worst mental illness episodes, the sufferers clearly feel—and at that moment are—out of control.

Certainly, Julie Schenecker, unlike many Americans, had access to mental health care from trained professionals. However, in many ways, their hands were tied, creating an obstacle to the provision of good, effective treatment. Most conclusions psychiatrists and psychologists reach are based on the self-reporting of their clients. In addition, the professionals are prevented from discussing these disclosures with the significant others in their patients' lives. Because of this restriction, it has been difficult to verify the accuracy of the clients' statements and it has crippled the ability of people like Parker to play an active role in their spouse's treatment and assessment. If there had been an open and forthright exchange of information between Parker and Julie's therapist, would it have enabled Parker to realize just how volatile the situation was before it was too late?

HIPAA was designed to protect a patient's privacy. Its goal has been to prevent abuses that could result from shared information. It seems clear that there needs to be some modification to the act—a way of guarding the patient's confidentiality, ensuring more effective treatment that could result from careful disclosure, and protecting the people around the patient, all at the same time. On the surface, believing we can balance those conflicting goals may sound idealistic and unrealistic. But if we don't make the attempt, we block the possibility of finding any reasons for these lethal actions and doom others, like Calyx and Beau, because of our rigidity.

Once we develop an understanding of the causes of maternal filicide, then we can be more aware of the danger signals sent out by neighbors, families, and friends. Every incident of physical abuse of a child needs to be reported and treated as the risk factor that it is. Every person with mental illness needs to be encouraged to get help and to be reassured that they will not be ostracized because of the chemical imbalances in their brains. They need to get the help deemed medically necessary and should not be forced to leave a facility prematurely because the health insurance company refuses more coverage based on the corporation's artificial, arbitrary, and stringent limitations. You cannot put a price tag on saving the life of a child.

While improving the current situation, we need to bear in mind that the majority of mentally ill patients pose no threat to their children. In helping the people who do, we need to be careful not to misjudge those who do not.

Acceptance of the reality of mental health problems does not imply excusing lethal behavior by anyone. Society—particularly its most defenseless members, like children—needs to be protected. Those who seek to do harm need to be separated from the rest of us. But more prevention through psychological counseling and psychiatric care can create an enormous reduction in the murders of children. Could any of us be opposed to that outcome?

How do we put Julie Schenecker into perspective? The mother whose murder of her child came closest to being like the crime committed by Julie was Stacey Pagli, who murdered her eighteen-year-old daughter less than a year before Julie's crime.

According to mental health experts on both sides of the case, Stacey was under extreme emotional duress on February 22, 2010. Her husband had repeatedly told her to go kill herself and that he didn't love her any longer.

When she came home from dropping a younger daughter at day care that morning, she started an argument with her daughter Marissa, an eighteen-year-old college freshman. The argument became physical after Marissa "mouthed off" at her. Stacey strangled her daughter to death, telling her it would be the last time she talked to her like that. She immediately attempted to end her own life by slitting her wrists and then by hanging.

She said to police, "I couldn't take it anymore. She couldn't talk to me like that." Stacey pled guilty to second-degree murder one week after Julie murdered Calyx and Beau. She received a twenty-year prison sentence.

Unlike Julie Schenecker, Stacey did not premeditate this crime. It was an impulsive act of rage. Stacey did not face a full trial and a jury decision. At this time, it appears that Julie will.

In essence, the jury will have to decide if Julie is an evil, psychopathic, cold-blooded murderer who deserves death or if she is insane enough or sufficiently mentally ill to deserve mercy. Both sides will carefully prepare their arguments and deliver them with a passionate intensity.

But as Dr. William Reid wrote in the *Journal of Psychiatric Practice:* "Juries are frightened by people who kill other people. They are very often even more frightened when defendants have mental illnesses and psychotic symptoms that they find horrible or unpredictable. The very factors that both clinicians and lawyers consider mitigating, and sometimes exculpating, may instead influence a jury to incarcerate the defendant or recommend execution."

The courtroom is certainly not a clinical environment where care is taken to understand each patient. Will the jury be able to set aside their fears and side with the defense theory of insanity? Will they follow the lead and opinion of the prosecution and send Julie to Death Row? Or will they choose a verdict and sentence lying somewhere in between the two extremes? Only time will tell.